LESSONS
from a
Girl's
Best
Friend

michelle mckinney hammond

HARVEST HOUSE PUBLISHERS

EUGENE, OREGON

Published in association with the literary agency of Alive Communications, Inc., 7680 Goddard Street, Ste #200, Colorado Springs, CO 80920. www.alivecommunications.com.

Cover photo © Tom Henry / Koechel Peterson & Associates

Cover by Koechel Peterson & Associates, Inc., Minneapolis, Minnesota

LESSONS FROM A GIRL'S BEST FRIEND
Copyright © 2008 by Michelle McKinney Hammond
Published by Harvest House Publishers
Eugene, Oregon 97402
www.harvesthousepublishers.com

Library of Congress Cataloging-in-Publication Data
McKinney Hammond, Michelle.
Lessons from a girl's best friend / Michelle McKinney Hammond.
    p. cm.
ISBN-13: 978-0-7369-2114-5 (pbk.)
ISBN-10: 0-7369-2114-1 (pbk.)
    1. McKinney Hammond, Michelle. 2. Christian biography—United States.
3. Dogs—Religious aspects—Christianity. 4. Human–animal relationships—Religious aspects. I. Title.
BR1725.M3568A3 2008
248.4—dc22
                                                            2008024130

Printed in the United States of America

08 09 10 11 12 13 14 15 / VP-SK / 11 10 9 8 7 6 5 4 3 2 1

Lord, You have made all creatures—
great and small—exceedingly wonderful.
Thank You for entrusting me
with two of Your precious creations.

To Milan and Matisse—
my two infinite sources of laughter and love.
I thank God for creating you.

To Annette Akers and Milo,
who introduced me to a wonderful life I knew not of!

Acknowledgments

They say it takes a village to raise a child, in this instance the same applies to this single, traveling girl when it comes to her dogs, so here goes:

🐾 To Daryl Martin (breeder extraordinaire) for giving me two of the most wonderful gifts I've ever received.

🐾 To Marilyn and Howard at *Good Dog,* along with John, Bobo, Lionel, Percy, Melvin, and all the teachers who have trained and continue to take such exceptional care of my babies. I always know they are in good hands when I leave them with you.

🐾 To John at *Clean Dog* and Barb at *Barker and Meowsky* for meticulously grooming my two children to look their best. Your perfectionism is showing.

🐾 To John and Phillip at *Tails in the City* for all the bling and fabulous things you bring into our lives.

🐾 To Tamara at *Petzercise,* JoAnne, and everyone else who add support to my world and make dog-rearing such an immense pleasure.

🐾 To all my family and friends who lovingly welcomed the new additions to my family.

🐾 To Nick Harrison and Barbara Gordon, my fine and patient editors. Thanks for keeping me on point. We clean up great together.

🐾 To Beth Jusino, my agent. Thank you for all you do. I appreciate your wise counsel and diligence. Thanks for listening too.

🐾 To my family at Harvest House, who always provoke me to keep stretching and digging deeper. I love and appreciate you all.

Contents

How It All Began

Take a look at that photo. That's me with Milan and Matisse. I still laugh when I think back through the years and realize how far I've come since the days when I didn't own a dog and certainly had no plans to acquire one.

Me with a dog? No way! Me with *two* dogs? Now that's a real laugh. But then something happened…something I never anticipated. God surprised me in a way I hadn't dreamed of. That's the story I want to tell you in this book. It's about how I started at "dogs are fine for *you,* but unless they do windows or perform some other beneficial function I don't see the point of owning one." I ended up not only adopting Milan and Matisse but *learning* from them. And not just about life, but about love and about God and the way He sees us. As the book title says, "Lessons from a girl's best friend."

Most of the important things in my life have been as a result of God's surprises. I never planned to be a single woman for so long. I never planned to leave my fast-paced job in the advertising world to become an author. Who knew I'd end up impacting the lives of women all over the world and even cohosting an Emmy award-winning television show! But now, more than a decade and 31 books later, I'm still amazed at the divine surprises that have changed my life and filled me with unexpected delight and satisfaction. Perhaps the biggest surprise of all is that I'm now writing a book about dogs, my beloved shih tzus Milan and Matisse.

Call me a hopeful romantic, but I've always believed in the power of love to heal, stimulate, and empower people to be their best. Love colors our world in various shades that affect our moods, the things we do and say, and how we live. Love can invite victory or chaos into our personal world. That's what got me writing in the first place. I was a miserable single, and my pain sent me on a mission to find joy. Through much self-reflection and realignment of attitudes, I emerged the better for it and ready to share my findings with others. That led to one book, and then another and another. Then the door opened for me to travel and speak all over the world.

For years now I've been meeting the most incredible people and discovering the amazing truth that no matter where I go, no matter what culture, gender, or age I address, everyone is wrestling with the same issues. It always comes back to the same age-old subject—love.

Everybody wants it, needs it, and is willing to go to extreme measures to get it. For me, a real turning point in learning about love came the day I decided to take the plunge into a relationship I wasn't sure I was ready for. But once I said yes there was no turning back. That was the day Milan came into my life. And the joy she brought was something no one could have convinced me of. Could something as simple as bringing a dog into my life really have that kind of impact? I would never have believed so. But it did.

This book is very personal. The lessons from Milan and Matisse have been so profound, I'm compelled to share them to bring more joy and insights to your life too. Interestingly, the lessons I've learned are not the kinds of things taught about God in a seminary or even in a Sunday morning sermon. No, they are more elemental...and often much funnier. Dogs make us laugh as they teach their lessons. It's my hope this book will bring some smiles, outright laughter, and perhaps a few tears as you meet Milan and Matisse...and discover some life truths that are sure to benefit you if you choose to embrace them.

1

The Wonder and Fear of It All

To be perfectly honest, before my love affair with my dogs began, pets of any persuasion—canine or otherwise—held no interest to me. For one thing, I was a commitment phobe. I assumed pets required upkeep, and I was too busy. Plus they were hairy, and I loved to wear black. They would not be a good wardrobe accessory or fit in with my home décor without causing a mess.

But even beyond all that, there was a deeper reason for me to disdain dogs. It goes back to my childhood, and my very first memory of a dog. I attended an all-girls school in Barbados. One day a German shepherd wandered onto the school grounds. At first my classmates and I were curious about this strange creature—the only thing in our midst that didn't look like us. And so we all gathered around for a closer inspection.

One of the bolder girls, Sharon, tentatively stuck out her finger toward the dog, who looked as if it didn't quite understand what she wanted him to do. Neither did we, yet Sharon persisted—taking little jabs toward the dog's snout while taunting our visitor with a sing-songy "Here, doggy, doggy," expecting some sort of response. Just what, none of us knew.

We didn't anticipate what happened next. It was like a nightmare.

One moment we were giggling and whispering; the next we were screaming in harmony with Sharon. Perhaps it was the dog's lack of understanding as to what it was he was expected to do with the wagging finger in front of his nose. Or maybe it was the little girl smell mingled with sweat that tempted him. For whatever reason, like a frog capturing a fly, that dog's teeth clamped down firmly on Sharon's juicy, inviting finger. At the sound of Sharon's blood-curdling shriek they opened just as quickly, releasing her finger, which was dangling as the blood freely flowed.

The air was immediately full of screams scaling operatic octaves somewhere in the soprano range of high C as we girls ran for cover, arms flailing in the air. We ran for a teacher, for safety, for what we didn't know. We just *ran*.

And then I think someone threw up.

Within moments a teacher (which one was hard to distinguish because my eyes were covered) scooped up Sharon and carried her away, leaving behind a bloody path toward the school infirmary.

The next day Sharon returned with her finger swathed in white. We all gathered to gaze at it reverently and ask in hushed tones about her welfare. The finger had been successfully stitched back. Later, after healing, Sharon was left with only two small scars to remind her where to keep her hands should she ever encounter a dog again.

I don't know what became of Sharon, but I do remember that the scar on my soul was larger than the scars on her finger. I certainly drew my impression of dogs from her experience, thankful that I had only been an observer of the lesson: *Dogs are to be feared and should not be trusted at close range.*

First impressions are lasting ones, and this traumatic encounter tempered my emotional response at my next canine experience. When I was in high school my family got a puppy. I don't recall how he came to be ours, but I do remember I named him Rico after the good-looking husband of one of my mother's friends. I had an adolescent crush on Monsieur Rigaud (that was his name, pronounced Ree-co), more enamored with his thick, wavy hair and heavy French accent than the actual man himself.

Rico was rather cute too. He was a cockapoo, champagne-colored with a white star on his forehead. Sadly, Rico's stay was cut unceremoniously short when he refused to be housebroken. No one in our house knew anything about training dogs. My mother's white carpeting was far more important than the patience required to train Rico when and where he was to relieve himself. Rico was given to a family friend, and that was the end of my second association with dogs. Now that I look back, I realize our lack of knowledge cost us at least 15 years of wonder that could have been ours, but instead this was enjoyed and reported to us by Rico's new owner.

One of my favorite authors, Donald Miller, wrote in *Blue Like Jazz* that sometimes we have to watch somebody else love something before we can love it ourselves. That was surely the case with me. But I wasn't there yet when it came to pets. Not by a long shot.

My next dog experience was with my hairdresser's small Maltese named Boopie. In my opinion Boopie proved to be more of an unnecessary diversion than a girl's best friend. Boopie registered in my mind as neither cute nor ugly—just a nuisance.

Every three months I liked to get my hair done. It took me about a week to condition myself mentally to make the appointment. Fixing my hair was a lengthy process, approximately 14 hours of sitting in the same spot while my hairdresser, Helen, carefully applied extensions, strands at a time, until my hair and her artistry are done. She performed her craft to perfection, but I always wondered how much shorter this ritual would have been if she didn't constantly stop and *pet* Boopie, *kiss* Boopie, *talk* to Boopie, *feed* Boopie snacks, and *walk* Boopie.

Boopie got on my nerves, okay?

Every now and then Boopie would sniff my feet and then walk away, knowing I had no special love for it (yes, I said *it!*). And it was right. As far as I was concerned Boopie was a distraction that stood between me and my beauty regimen. Of course I could never voice my lack of affection for Boopie to my hairdresser or I would lose her. Boopie was her child, her *everything,* and if someone didn't like it, well, that person could just find another hairdresser. No amount of money was worth the disdain of her beloved Boopie.

I found her devotion a bit...no, a lot much. She needed to get a life! Her love for her dog revealed that she had "issues"—issues that I certainly didn't have.

That was before my own conversion to born-again dog lover.

In my wildest dreams I couldn't picture my life, my choices, or my personal disciplines being controlled by a dog. I played along with my hairdresser's obsession with Boopie and feigned mild interest to acquire my desired end—fabulous tresses. Sometimes we have to tolerate the passions of others to get what we want, I reasoned. As long as I didn't have to take Boopie home, we could coexist for a time. I could even extend a detached pat on its head from time to time, but that's as far as I would go.

I had no positive reference point about dogs, only two negatives that filtered my understanding of Helen's love for Boopie into a caricature I couldn't relate to. Little did I know that my prejudice against dogs—though understandable given my experiences—was delaying me from unimaginable delights and blessings.

🐾 Paws to Reflect 🐾

Many people don't understand how someone can love a God they can't see. How can an invisible God be involved in our daily decisions? How can He really affect our lives at all? "If God exists," they reason, "He is best kept at arm's length. To know Him might prove to be a distraction, not a blessing."

Sometimes people may recall a bad experience, either as a child or in their early adult years, that left them suspicious or turned off toward God—just as I was turned off toward dogs. Or perhaps people have had negative experiences with someone who claimed to represent God. They may have decided that if God was like *this* person, forget it. Or maybe they got the impression from this person that God was angry at them, perhaps vindictive, waiting to bash them over the head the minute they made the slightest mistake or did something wrong.

These types of experiences leave deep impressions in human souls akin to the track marks left by four-wheelers in the mud after a rainy day, grooves that leave devastation and lasting damage unless they are repaired and restored. Open wounds fester and make surviving trials and the weighty matters of life difficult. All that remains is the injury, making it difficult for many to embrace the idea of a loving God with His hand outstretched toward them in love and compassion.

If it's true, and it is, that the fear of the Lord is the beginning of wisdom...how did we make "fear" something so far removed from the deep respect and awe it's intended to be? How did the fear of the Lord become the straightjacket some people call Christianity?

Perhaps we've misinterpreted the context of the word "fear" and misconstrued the true meaning of the verse in Proverbs that says, "The fear of the LORD is the beginning of wisdom, and knowledge of the Holy One is understanding" (9:10).

A healthy sense of "reverent wonder," as Eugene Peterson, paraphraser of The Message Bible, would say, gives us a breathtaking view of an all-powerful, omniscient God who is bigger than us and all our problems. Knowledge of who He is and how much He loves us gives us clarity on why He says what He says in His Word, the Bible. It also makes us joyful, willing, and obedient lovers of the One who loves us most.

We are so loved and protected by God that we can possess a peace that passes all understanding—no matter what's going on around us. Yet sadly, so many people needlessly struggle. Their fear of God paralyzes them from embracing the liberty that can be found in a relationship with Him, and they become more like religious robots who are so strictly spiritual they are no earthly good.

Another sad option is that the lack of understanding of the heart and motives of God reduces some people to a bad reflection of who Christ is, repelling the world and making a relationship with God totally undesirable—kind of like my response to Boopie, whom I later came to appreciate and love too late. (He's now in doggie heaven.)

People who are bound by fear or lack understanding, like I did about what a dog could bring into my world, can never understand the joy that could be theirs through something that *seems* to demand more than it has to give. We fail to realize that we're bigger than our fears. To *understand* we have the power to set our fears aside and accept the love that's waiting for us—God's goodness.

It is clearly evident to me now. Fear and a lack of understanding are nothing more than dangerous robbers…thieves of pleasure as well as eternity.

2

The Value of Good Neighbors

I was so excited! I'd finally become a home owner. A real adult. For years I avoided the issue. I suppose it had something to do with my hopes of a "knight in shining armor" suddenly appearing over the horizon of my Cinderella dreams, sweeping me off my feet, carrying me away to the perfect house he'd purchased just for me…where I settled into being a very happy, undesperate housewife. And we both lived happily ever after.

But that didn't happen.

So when my friends decided to stage an intervention, suggesting I grow up, wake up, and smell the coffee, I put away my childish notions and went in search of my very first home. For several years I had looked longingly at a beautiful, historical warehouse nestled on a bridge that crosses the Chicago River. How perfect it would be if some real estate developer would get my vision and convert that warehouse into loft apartments. It wasn't Plan A (the knight in shining armor), but it was a perfect Plan B.

And then one day it happened!

The signs went up, the conversion went into full gear, and one year later I was finally moving into my new digs, complete with the high ceilings and ebony-stained floors I had dreamed of. To top things off, I was even able to wrangle an unbelievably great deal on my purchase. For me that was a final stamp of approval from God that indeed I was doing the right thing.

Everything was perfect. I'd already met one of my neighbors—an opera singer. I'd been told there was also a basketball player in the building, as well as one of Oprah's assistants. I was truly in exceptional company, which could only translate to a fine quality of life in my very own home—and marked profitability as my home appreciated in the years to come.

Little did I know I had other neighbors I wouldn't find so desirable. Neighbors of the four-legged kind. Neighbors that pooed and piddled in the hallways. My dream home quickly morphed into an environment that caused me great concern. My image of a perfect utopia and future profits was quickly dwindling.

Something had to be done. Why didn't the owners of these canine pests housebreak their pets? "After all," I reasoned, "we humans have to wait until we get to a bathroom. Why can't dogs hold it? What would happen if we all went wherever we wanted to?" I sniffed. So off to a homeowner's association meeting I went, determined to have them find a solution to this intolerable situation.

Needless to say, I hadn't anticipated the passion of the dog owners in question. But just as passionate were those of us who didn't appreciate dog droppings in the hallways. And so two opposing camps were formed: those who demanded the removal of all dogs from the building and the Doggy Board for Animal Rights, as I came to call them.

The problem, according to the dog owners, was there was really no convenient place for all these dogs to "do their business." The planters in front of the building were off limits because no one wanted a smelly entrance. Although a doggy park was under construction nearby, it was at least a block away and was presently unfinished. The grass that stretched endlessly around the building across the street was off limits and adorned with "No dog walking! Private property!" signs. This meant dogs had to walk practically two blocks before reaching a place where they could relieve themselves. Add to that the fact that many of the dogs had to wait until their owners got home from work, and it was clear this was an "accident" waiting to happen for many a pooch.

Still, it was *their* problem not mine. Although I tried to muster a bit of sympathy as I envisioned those poor dogs rushing with crossed legs toward the nearest patch of available ground, I determined that no one was going to ruin the hallways in my newly acquired property. Not on my watch! No way, no how!

The battle raged on with no resolution in sight. As a result, anarchy reigned. Some of the dog owners marched their dogs across the street, ignoring the signs and garnering the resentment of the neighbors who lived there (even though those neighbors themselves ignored the signs and freely walked their dogs on the restricted grass). Meanwhile, as tensions were mounting, the piddle and poo stains were increasingly polka-dotting the carpeting in the hallways at an alarming rate.

With no solution forthcoming, I decided to pray about it.

Okay, so maybe I'm the first person to pray about doggie poo… but I was getting desperate. My prayer was pretty straightforward: "Lord, I want You to remove all the dogs from the building. They are *ruining* our property. I'm trying to guard the investment You've made available to me, but the devil is peeing all over it!"

Yes, it was spiritual warfare! When I look back now, I smile at my determination to cast all the dogs out of the building through prayer. A doggy exorcism.

So there I was. Praying, praying, praying about this problem… and then I heard the strangest response to my prayers. It was *not* the answer I expected…or wanted. God never addressed the concerns I voiced. He simply said, "Michelle, I want you to get a dog."

At first I thought I was hearing things. Surely the devil, with his sick sense of humor, had somehow managed to intercept my prayers and offer this twisted solution. So I rebuked my unwelcome visitor and pressed back into prayer. Again the answer came, "Michelle, I want you to get a dog." This made no sense! Yet I couldn't shake this impression that I, Miss Get-These-Dogs-Out-of-My-Building was to acquire a four-legged beast myself. As the weeks rolled by, this disturbing thought became a weight on my soul.

In an effort to solicit an objective opinion, I ran this idea by several of my closest friends. Every one of them was sure what I was hearing was *not* from God. They all thought I was suffering from some sort of delusion. "God would never tell you to get a dog," they said. One of my closest male friends even said it wasn't *my* welfare he was concerned about, it was the dog's! "Don't do that to a dog!" he said. They all rationalized that my travel schedule alone should be a large enough reason for me to abandon this crazy notion. "You're never home," they said. "Exactly how would you take care of it?"

Of course I was happy to accept all of their reasons for why getting a dog was the worst idea on the planet for me. Acquiring a dog was certainly not my choice anyway. I took their words as confirmation that indeed the devil was messing with me. I felt released to move on. No dog for me. My friends had confirmed it.

Meanwhile my angst over the state of the hallways was growing as more and more dogs moved into the building. Big dogs, little dogs, boy dogs, girl dogs all conspired against my hopes for living in a home with nice, clean, attractive hallways.

Still I was haunted by the voice that would not go away: "Michelle, get a dog." The thought sat on my head like the heavy tome used for practicing good posture "back in the day." I woke in the middle of the night hearing the refrain. Yet I wouldn't relent. Like Saul, who later was transformed and renamed Paul, on the way to Damascus, who was bent on annihilating all the Christians from the face of the earth, I was intent on getting all the demon dogs out of my building.

I didn't care where they went—just *out of my building*. And I certainly didn't understand why all those dog owners were so committed to these creatures. I mean, these people *loved* their dogs! This was no mild emotion. We're talking deep commitment here. Their beloved pets were "family" to them…at the expense of others, in my opinion. I just didn't get it. But more important, I didn't feel they had the right to make their love affair intrude on *my* world.

To make matters worse, these dog enthusiasts did a good job of making everyone else feel guilty about their dilemma. I really didn't like that part. I felt that I was becoming a victim of their passion. Why couldn't they just have their dogs and leave me alone? I shouldn't be made to feel as if I were evil just because I wasn't interested in their pets—petting them, speaking to them, or caring where and how they piddled.

The solution for me was simple. They could keep their dogs as long as it didn't affect the welfare of anything concerning me—and that included my surroundings. As long as I was unaware that I was amid dogs we could all abide in peace together. That would settle the matter in my book.

Or so I thought.

🐾 Paws to Reflect 🐾

Have you encountered Christians or others who are adamant about their personal causes? You know the type—the ones who weigh us down with condemnation if we don't believe what they believe and how they believe with the same fervency they have. They can make us feel like we're totally out of the loop, not with it, uninformed, misguided. In short, we feel horrible. If we're talking about faith, we can end up feeling like the biggest sinners in the world or like we don't love Jesus enough.

For those who haven't entered into a relationship with God the feeling of condemnation can be even deeper as "Christians" make them feel they're wrong for not joining the club. More often than not, this "truth" about Jesus isn't delivered with much love, causing the ones on the receiving end to feel that surely they're headed straight to hell in a handbasket unless they line up with the principles and beliefs of the ones who are insisting they embrace salvation and reformation. I dare say that most of the time the poor victims of this type of pressure spend more time defending themselves than really being open to hearing the Good News that is usually lost amid the threats, accusations, and condemnation.

As I reflect on this, I remember that when I became a Christian

I didn't really know any other Christians. No one had "witnessed" to me. I simply prayed the sinner's prayer at home alone in my bed after reading a very profound little book called *The Late Great Planet Earth.*

By the time I met other Christians, I knew enough to be convicted about my sinful lifestyle just from their presence. They didn't have to say anything. Their godliness illuminated my ungodliness and made me *want* to change.

I sometimes wonder if I had met some of those militant Christians before I accepted Christ, would I have wanted what they had? Maybe not. I say this because later I found some Christians rather obnoxious in the way they shared their faith. Their passion made them emotional without enough rational information to substantiate their fervency, and I had a lot of trouble with that. Fortunately I learned to sidetrack these types of people early and go directly to God for the information I was seeking about who He wanted me to be.

Passion is a powerful thing. Sometimes the passion of others can make us very uncomfortable because it demands a response from us, from everyone who witnesses it, whether we agree or not. It pricks us and makes us examine ourselves, searching for what is wrong with us—whether anything is or not.

The apostle Paul tried to silence the voices that were echoing what God's voice had been saying to him for some time. He sought to kill the messengers because the message became too overwhelming for him. But the day came when God's message got through loud and clear: "Hey, Saul! Cut it out! Why are you persecuting My people? Don't you know that by picking on them you are really hurting Me? You're picking a fight you can't win. Now get up and do as I say!" Paul quickly learned that the very thing he was trying to squelch was the very thing he had been searching for.

In the same way God said to me, "Michelle, stop picking on the dog owners and do what I told you to do."

"But why, Lord?" I cried. "I don't understand why You want me to get a dog!"

He went on to tell me that He was going to use the dog in my life to refine me. He told me I had grown selfish and self-consumed, that I needed to learn to take care of someone other than myself.

Uh-oh. No wonder I didn't want to hear what God was saying. I didn't want anyone or anything changing my life or my agenda. But God is seldom moved by what we don't want. He knows what He's planned is the best for us. He told me I needed discipline in my life. I was like a gypsy floating from moment to moment. This is not the practice of someone who is successful in life.

Life requires order, discipline, and routine. For this reason God had instituted sunrise, sunset, and the four seasons. Some things in the universe are deliberately and entirely predictable, creating a wonderful mix with the randomness that happens without warning or invitation.

As a single person not tied to the demands of a mate, I was used to doing as I pleased, when I pleased. I answered to no one but myself… and God. Since God isn't visible to the naked eye, I could ignore Him if His instructions weren't convenient to my desires at the time. Are you shocked by that statement? Let's face it: We all go there from time to time. If I were to be honest with myself and God, I had to admit it was true that I'd become a spoiled and willful drifter, capricious in nature. There was no pull, no reason for me to have an agenda carved in stone, to dash home at any given time, to stop working, to have a meal, to exercise, or even to rest. My body was confused. It didn't know what to expect on any given day, and the effects of my random living were taking their toll.

Once, after being bed-bound for an extended time after an automobile accident and doing everything in my bed, I had to go to therapy because I was having trouble sleeping. I was told I couldn't do anything in my bed but sleep. I couldn't talk on the phone, watch TV, read, eat—*nothing.* Nothing but sleep. My entire system had to be reprogrammed to understand that the bed was only for sleeping. And just as the spirit of man was made for God to give Him fellowship and pleasure, the soul was created to reflect God's order. Without cooperating with this invisible law of the universe, our lives are fitful, unrestful, and chaotic.

I couldn't argue with God about that. My life was a living, breathing example of being out of order.

About the time of this great revelation or "Damascus road experience," I met a woman in the park walking her dog—a miniature collie. I stopped to ask a question about her little companion. She seemed quite happy to answer. In fact, the floodgates opened, and she went on to tell me how getting a dog was the best thing she'd ever done. Her friends warned her she was crazy to consider getting a dog because, like me, she traveled so much. But she ignored their advice and adopted this beautiful collie. As a result, she was a different person. She told me she now had greater order and discipline than ever before. She was on a schedule that improved the quality of her life. Acquiring a dog had made the difference.

I listened in fascination. Had she been listening in on my prayers? Overhearing my conversations with God? She was certainly seconding His motion to get a dog.

As I walked away, I wasn't quite convinced yet. I had kind of gotten into being a verbal pet slayer, but I was beginning to waver. I considered the fact that a lack of order creates chaos, which holds no good for those who reap the sad results of a life spinning out of control—and that was certainly me. As boring as it sounded, I had to agree with God that it is the predictability of life that anchors the soul and makes stable human beings who go on to meaningful accomplishments that please Him and bless others.

The things we must do on a regular basis—eat, drink, sleep, breathe, love, interact with God—though they may seem boring at times, are the mundane necessities that feed and nourish us best. Like a bland diet, they may not always taste that great but they sustain our system and settle our hearts, securing them for the journey ahead and fortifying us with sustained power. And who wouldn't want that?

Order and discipline were beginning to sound better by the minute.

SoundBite
Keeping It Simple

Far too many times I've been envious of the life Milan and Matisse lead. They know their schedule and prefer that it not be circumvented. They find comfort in the mundane. There is safety in routine. They know what to expect in life. They know they will take a stroll in the morning, gaze at the river, chase seagulls, leaves, whatever catches their eyes and then return home for a savory breakfast followed by a meet-and-greet session with anyone who happens by my office. Next they'll settle into their beds for a nice nap, after which they'll be ready for another leisurely stroll.

After dutifully doing their midday business they'll come back to the office, have a treat, take another nap, and then wake up to inform me it's time to go home for supper. After dining we take another stroll around the neighborhood and enjoy a nice visit with all the other dogs and parents out for an evening stretch. This outing can last for at least an hour, depending on who we meet along the way. Then it's back home to settle in for the evening. After one more bout of playtime, everyone is reasonably exhausted and ready to call it another day.

Simple. No drama. No harrowing surprises.

I wish my life was like that.

I'm often asked what a typical day looks like in my life. I always laugh when someone asks that because there is no such thing. I've often thought my life should be a reality show—but no one would believe it. "Drama, drama, drama" is all I can say. Whether it's mine or someone I know, it's always an adventure with most of the story taking unanticipated turns. There is much to be said for keeping things simple, knowing what to expect, and feeling safe.

My mentor once said that men are like that. They want three things: to be well fed, well loved, and well respected. This completes a man. Females seem to be considerably more complicated. Perhaps this makes us our own worst enemies.

Someone once suggested it's not the struggles that make us question God, it's the drudgery of everyday life...and yet we pray to be delivered from all the complexities we struggle with.

God isn't as complicated as we make Him. His list of what He desires is actually very short. He knows what He wants, and He doesn't get distracted. He wants *us*—to love and to cherish us in an intimate, passionate way for eternity. And that, my friends, is simple enough.

3

The Phenomenon of Focus

As I was struggling over whether getting a dog was right for me, I began to develop an interest in the annual kennel club dog shows that aired over the Thanksgiving holiday weekend.

My mother's kitchen was the place to congregate as Thanksgiving smells filled the room. Plus she had a little television in her breakfast nook. I loved to settle in, enjoy the company of my relatives, and watch the dog show while waiting for the first taste of whatever was simmering on the stove. Life was fine. My mother's kitchen provided a real comfort moment. We would sit watching as various beautifully groomed dogs trotted proudly in front of the cameras. I especially loved the "toy class" of dogs. I found myself becoming quite knowledgeable on the different breeds of dogs, making notes on the ones I would like to investigate further—*IF* I should ever finally listen to God and stop resisting the pull to actually get a four-legged companion.

It was fascinating to see the variety of dogs and hear their stories. One was a herder, another a hunter. Each breed had a different function and, based on how they were bred, their behavior and habits were generally predictable. This is very important for an owner to know because the last thing a quiet person would want is a hyper dog requiring a lot of physical activity. Apartment dwellers wouldn't want to get a dog that requires wide open spaces to roam. That wouldn't be fair to the animal.

So there I sat, munching a fresh, hot roll and taking notes on the various breeds promenading in their splendor. What I was going to do with this information was still up in the air, but at least if I did decide to get a dog, I'd be making an educated choice.

I remember thinking, *If I had done this much research on the men I dated before I invested my heart into them, perhaps I could have saved myself a lot of heartbreak over the years!* When I think about it, it's quite easy to fall in love with puppies because they're all so cute (kind of like men), but then they grow up and things change. Sometimes they're not so cute anymore, and they develop habits that are less than desirable. But by then you're stuck in a commitment that may be difficult to extricate from.

Over the years I've come to believe dating is not for mating but rather for collecting data. Forget getting caught up in the chemistry and losing your objectivity so you don't exercise the sense God gives you. During a season of dating, one should be gathering the necessary data to determine if the potential partner might be future spouse material. Or at least finding out if the relationship is worth investing more time and emotional commitment. It's not enough to know that a guy is cute or that I like him right now. Will I like him *later* is the question. After the cuteness wears off, what's left behind the haze of hormones and the things we do to impress one another initially? Is there great character behind that polished facade? Is there the ability to commit? What is his history? His values? What are his friends and family like?

Dog experts say that when selecting a dog it's important to know the family line. Are they purebreds? Mutts? Champions? They suggest you visit the dog a couple of times to see how it behaves. If he's all over the place in his pen, he'll be all over the place at your house. You can train dogs, but you can't change their temperaments. Though many a woman has tried to change and "fix" a man, it's true to say that doesn't work either.

My conclusion? If people checked out their potential mates the way we do our homework on dogs, jobs, real estate—you name it—perhaps we would make better choices and enjoy more lasting relationships. Hmmm…I'm talking to myself here, but if the shoe fits…

Back to Thanksgiving. There were several dogs from the toy breeds that got my attention, particularly the Maltese and the shih tzu. I thought they were so cute! And I liked the fact they seemed to know it. They floated around the ring like prom queens, their flowing locks blowing in the breeze behind them like elegant skirts, their top knots fashionably in place, acting as if they had been groomed to walk the red carpet on Oscar night. I'm sure if they could wave they would.

On further investigation I discovered that shih tzus were pretty much considered royalty. The story goes they were bred for the emperor of China; commoners weren't allowed to own them. Their job was to simply look pretty and beautify the palace, which they did in true regal fashion. So stately and sedate were they that if they barked at anyone that person was considered evil and ordered executed! Paintings and statues paying tribute to their beauty were everywhere, all of which no doubt solidified in their little minds that they were created to be adored, pampered, and admired—nothing more, nothing less.

Another surprising result of watching dog shows was that I became more aware of the dogs around me. Driving down the street I began to be more observant when I saw a dog. And it seemed I had developed a special homing instinct for shih tzu and other little fluffy dogs. I'd never noticed how many there were before, but all of a sudden the world was filled with these little beauties. It's amazing how a new awareness opens the world and fine-tunes focus. Have you ever noticed once you fall in love with a certain type of car you start seeing it everywhere? It's as if our focus attracts the very thing we've committed our hearts and desires to. Makes you wonder what would happen if we made finding love or accomplishment or any good or bad thing our main pursuit, doesn't it?

Focus is magnetic and revelatory. It exposes what our spirits are really longing for. I'm talking about the stuff that gets buried under our intellect. The stuff we rationalize away because it just doesn't make sense. And yet every time we encounter that thing—whether it be a dog, a baby, a success story, a couple strolling in the park that stirs up your desire for a love that looks like theirs, the peace you see on someone's face that magnifies your own desire to find a quiet place in your own soul—we've got to pay attention. I believe that focus is God's way of compelling us toward the things that will make us whole. When we allow ourselves to be distracted from our true heart's cry, our joy and fulfillment are siphoned off and we're left with endless, unanswered questions about life, ourselves, and God.

🐾 Paws to Reflect 🐾

Could it be that the clues for meaning you look for in life are not the things that scream loudly, interrupting your original thoughts? Maybe it's the still, small voice within that keeps pointing with determination at the one thing that is the sure solution to your deepest needs. That's what it was like for me when I finally found God. But first I had to get past all the noise and futile suggestions that deepened my unrest. All the voices that were like commercials interrupting my train of thought. You know how it goes. Commercials can pull your thoughts in another direction. Their invitations can make you forget what you were centered on. "Now where was I?" you say. Or "What was going on before they cut in?" Perhaps it was a food commercial, and suddenly you're hungry. Without knowing why, you find yourself in the kitchen scrounging for snacks and you miss the end of the show. You wonder about the conclusion of the matter! This is life.

What you're really looking for and the things that can get you off course aren't so obvious at times. But you keep coming back to the same place, looking for what has been misplaced among your efforts at survival. And when you finally follow whatever, you focus on the path that leads you home to the place of your desires. Here's an important caveat: Sometimes the address is not what you expect.

As you might guess, all this time I was becoming (much to my surprise) attracted to dogs. Yes, I was officially and finally being sucked into the doggy world.

Before I knew it, there was no turning back.

It was as inevitable as salvation is for anyone searching for true peace and joy.

I was getting a dog.

4

The Law of Attraction

When I first moved into my building all of the units weren't yet finished, so it hadn't reached full occupancy. Perhaps this made those of us who settled in early a little more social than we otherwise might have been. People in a big city have a way of living in close quarters without ever acknowledging one another's presence. One day, while in pursuit of a parking space, I became acquainted with the president of the condo board and his lovely wife. She loved to cook and I loved to eat, so we hit it off right away. We bonded over many meals, exchanging gossip about the progress of the construction and the politics between the developer and the condo board. It was really juicy stuff.

Besides this couple, I knew only one other person in the building: a very cute opera singer down the hall from me. We bonded over decorating tips and, of course, food. It was the first time in my city-dwelling life that I didn't eat alone most evenings. We all floated from unit to unit, sharing dinners with one another and commiserating over the progress of the building and speculating on new neighbor sightings.

Then one day I stopped in my tracks as I entered the building. A woman was passing me on her way out the door, and she was holding the most adorable puppy I'd ever seen. He looked like a teddy bear…a miniature Ewok. There he sat nestled in his owner's arms, loving the ride as if he were a prince enjoying homage by one of his subjects.

At that moment something happened to me that had never

happened before. Completely ignoring the woman, I dove toward her cherished fluff ball, grabbing his whiskers on both sides of his face as I squealed in delight. "Oh my goodness," I squeaked. "You are the cutest thing I've ever seen. Hello, precious!"

The dog merely looked at me and batted his eyelashes—which had to be two inches long. I'm sure he said, "Hey, I know I'm cute, but calm down, lady!" Meanwhile his owner was beaming proudly, enjoying the attention her little pooch was receiving.

That was the moment I was pushed over the edge. I just *had* to have a dog exactly like this one. I knew it then and there. I wanted that specific breed, whatever it was. And surprise of surprises—he was a shih tzu and his name was Milo. Milo's owner, whom I later learned was Annette, excused herself, explaining that if my admiration continued any longer Milo's bladder would explode.

After her departure and on my way up to my place, I realized I'd failed to ask her where she got her perfect specimen of a dog. I went back to the doorman and left a note for her to call me and give me the name and number of Milo's breeder.

Two weeks later I still hadn't seen Milo or heard from Annette. The doorman told me she was traveling, so I was left to go in search of a cute shih tzu on my own.

A friend of mine named Bill, who is an avid dog lover (in fact, the only dog lover among all my friends), suggested I go on the American Kennel Club website to find reputable breeders. "Otherwise you don't know what you'll be getting." He sniffed. Bill is the owner of a rather elegant whippet named Cyril, who had been imported all the way from Kentucky or Paris, I can't remember which, but what I do remember is that Cyril comes from a lengthy lineage of champions and don't you forget it!

So to the website I went, searching for breeders in my area. I narrowed my search to three and called them. The first breeder assured me her puppies came house ready, totally potty trained. That appealed to me but I wanted more information. On to the next breeder I went. His name was Larry. Larry said he bred champions, and as a matter of fact he would be showing some of his finest dogs at a show in Wisconsin that very weekend. Other than that he was quite standoffish and a bit evasive. However, I agreed to meet him at the dog show and find out more, even though I wasn't really feeling the love from Larry. The final number I dialed was for a lady named Daryl, who grilled me like I was applying to adopt a child. I got in no questions; she asked them all.

"Where do you live?"

"What type of work do you do?"

"Do you have any children?"

"How do you intend to take care of a dog when you're away at work?"

When I said I traveled a lot, Daryl sounded hesitant. She said the only way she would allow one of her dogs to become mine was if I agreed to bring it back to board with her when I traveled because she didn't approve of kennels. I was a bit taken aback but conceded. Daryl then told me she was also showing dogs at the same show as Larry, so we agreed to meet at the doggie fair grounds. I would follow up with an appointment the following Monday to see her dogs where she housed them.

Fellow dog lover Bill was on for the trip, so off we went to Wisconsin on a bright and early Saturday morning. It seemed only right that he go with me. Bill had always been around for serious milestone decisions in my life, helping me to make wise choices. He was with me when I bought my first piece of serious jewelry, helping me with the selection. He announced it was time for me to grow up and become a responsible adult, ushering me into home ownership. He pooh-poohed my selections on apartments he deemed unsafe or unfit for me to live in, and he helped me select my first home and even helped me get the loan. He was my realtor! He also advised against the suitors he said were "unworthy" of me. So now it was only natural that he also be the one to help me select my first dog.

Once we made it to the highway (after a brief detour to our favorite suburban mall), we were off—until we ran into a huge traffic jam.

Winding along at a snail's pace, our hour-and-a-half trip turned into a four-hour meander. By the time we got to the dog show, Larry was gone. Bill suggested that I ask if anyone knew Daryl. "If a breeder is any good, they will all know her," he said. Sure enough, everyone knew her and pointed me in her direction.

After introducing myself, Daryl told me she knew Larry and was, in fact, showing his dogs along with a little Maltese who was being groomed in preparation for her promenade around the ring. When I asked to see Larry's dogs, Daryl led me back to the crates where the dogs were being kept and allowed me to peer in. Nothing suited my fancy. They didn't look like Milo. She studied my face and said with just a slight bit of haughtiness, "You don't have to make up your mind today." Her chin lifted higher. "*My* dogs don't look like his."

I took the hint. Now I was completely curious to see what her dogs looked like.

After meeting with Daryl, Bill and I wandered around the grounds and took in the sights. These people were part of a world I knew nothing of. They were deeply engaged in their dogs. Suddenly I felt very shallow. I wasn't sure I could be this committed. I was still stuck on cute; that was as far as I had gotten in my mindset. Walking, feeding, training...all the words blurred together. Did I really want to be *this* involved?

On the way home Bill voiced his concern at having been gone so long from his beloved Cyril. I realized Bill was one of the committed ones. For me, I had Milo's cute face looming before me, asking me in a singing voice, "Don't you want me, baby? Don't you want me? Ooooh, oh, oh oh..."

And indeed I did, but to be perfectly honest, I wanted the pleasure without the responsibility. I liked the idea of attracting the admiration of passersby as I walked my cute little fluff ball. The idea of having a real live teddy bear was also highly desirable. It was the rest of the package that put my heart on pause. This was when it dawned on me that I was a hopeless commitment phobe. I thought of the movie *28 Days*, where the test to see if the recovering substance abusers were ready for relationships was if they could keep a pet or a plant alive for one year. At this point I felt I would fail miserably.

To be honest, it wasn't just the dog thing. It was also romantic relationships, buying real estate, signing on the dotted line for anything that even *hinted* at long-term commitment. All these things caused me to break out in a sweat.

I remember after writing my first book my publisher asked me what I wanted to write next and my first thought was, *You mean I have to keep this up?* If I almost lost it over a publishing deal, just think of the trepidation that swept over me at the thought that I was going to be responsible for something that was going to be totally dependant on me for yeee-ars!

🐾 Paws to Reflect 🐾

I also thought in terms of my relationship with God. Have I wanted all the benefits of salvation without the commitment of nurturing my relationship with God? Even worse, could it be possible that I didn't want the responsibility of the follow-up to anything He said? Now I was beginning to see why God had been telling me, "Michelle, get a dog." I was selfish. I was a taker. What was going to make me change? Wanting something I didn't have more than what I already had.

It's said that until the pain of staying the same is greater than the pain of change, people won't change. I wanted to come home to someone…or something…that would be happy to see me after I'd been out and about absorbing the love of my readers and sharing with those who came to hear me speak. Being alone always seemed magnified after my trips. This led me to the conclusion that I wanted love in my life more than coming home to a loudly silent house. Suddenly the leverage of Milo's cuteness was greater than my reluctance to take responsibility for something other than myself. I wanted what Annette had.

When I'd taken my eyes off Milo long enough to acknowledge Annette, there was such joy and peace in her countenance, and I knew Milo was the source of it. Milo made me want my own Milo.

Something about how Annette was enjoying her little love bug made me obsessed with experiencing that same joy.

🐾 Paws to Reflect 🐾

I think a lot of Christians could take a clue from this. I've come to the conclusion that Jesus is not the problem with some aspects of Christianity—*Christians* are. Long after I became a Christian, I struggled with some of my fellow believers—with their attitudes toward one another's imperfections, with their elitist bearing toward those they considered "uncircumcised Philistines." I confess that I had "been there, done that" until I realized it wasn't working. I had to come to the place of realizing, "There, but for the grace of God, go I," and how! This led me to conclude that we as Christians can do a far better job of making the world want what we have. But that means we actually have to *enjoy* our relationship with God, *relish* living by faith, and *revel* in the truths that God shares in His Word. Only with that enthusiasm can we interest others. Some Christians struggle with making their faith look attractive because they fail to fully realize the beauty of what they hold.

The most incredible gift in the world has been made to look like a virus to be feared rather than a cure to be desired. What happened to inspiring others to want to live a better life? Whatever happened to making knowing God look downright awesome?

Think about it! Once you get religion out of the way and go back to what Jesus offers—which is a personal, intimate relationship with God—what is there *not* to want? Everyone wants to be at peace with God. Everyone wants the assurance that God is on his or her side. Everyone wants unconditional love. Everyone wants the joy and peace God promises and the eternal security He offers.

What people *don't* want is a religion that makes them feel as if they're choking to death. Love just doesn't do that...but religion can. Religion constricts. But love is something else. Love is caught up in love itself. So much so that it becomes contagious. Love pulls you out of your present insistences. It changes you without coercion. It calls you to give without considering the cost. It entices you to give of yourself with complete abandon, so intoxicated are you with the presence of the one you love.

Milo brought this home to me. He was a completely huggable bundle of love uninterrupted by any other agenda. And that is also what God is.

Suddenly the responsibility of commitment didn't seem like so much work after all.

5

The Magnitude of Decision

The decision had been made, but I knew I would still need moral support, so off to Daryl-the-breeder's house I went with my friend Nancy. Nancy knew I was still nervous about taking the final step toward puppy commitment. I knew her encouraging me all the way would help me over the last hump of trepidation. Winding over hill, dale, and freeway, we finally found Daryl's house nestled on a tree-lined street in a very nice neighborhood about an hour outside of Chicago.

Daryl greeted me, sizing me up again as I entered her home. We were also met by a chorus of barks in a full range of pitches. She truly lived with her dogs!

Leading me to a back bedroom, she proudly flung open the door to reveal pens holding several puppies, along with their nursing mothers. She held up a tiny little baby girl the size of her hand.

"Isn't she lovely?" she asked.

I stared at the dog. The dog stared back at me. Both of us were speechless. Daryl continued holding her aloft—and just out of touching range. She had already warned me that I couldn't touch her because she hadn't had her shots yet. In fact, if I wanted her, she wouldn't be ready for another two months.

"This one is going to be petite," Daryl said. "I thought of you because you said you would like to be able to travel with your dog."

"I think I'll call her Paris." The voice came from somewhere outside my head. I was surely having some kind of out-of-body experience. After gently setting Paris back down in her pen, Daryl led me back to the living room. I looked back to see Paris' mother looking at me very sadly, as if already accusing me of taking her child from her. I felt guilty. Numbly I wrote my deposit check and handed it over.

Daryl eyed me again. "Are you sure you want to do this?"

Nancy chimed in, "Ooh yes, this decision has been a year in the making. Trust me, she's ready!"

I tried to match the smile on Nancy's face while seconding the motion. "Oh yes, I'm definitely ready."

The rest of Daryl's instructions regarding when the dog would be ready, what I would need to bring, and recommendations for her care totally went in one ear and out the other. I was still stuck on the fact that I had actually signed a check for a real dog!

Nancy gently guided me out the door, knowing I needed help. As we settled into my car she suggested that perhaps a wonderful dinner would help me get over my shock. "I can't believe you're doing this!" she chortled.

I thought she was getting a little too much enjoyment out of this. We stopped for dinner, and after the first bite of pasta, I remembered that if I wanted to change my mind I still had two months to get out of the deal...although something told me that wouldn't be happening.

Two months sped by and then one day, close to the date that I was supposed to bring little Paris home, I received a cryptic voice mail from Daryl. "Call me. I need to talk to you."

Something told me this was not good. By now I had built up a healthy anticipation of Paris' coming home. I'd bonded with Annette and Milo over *America's Top Model,* along with dinner every week, and was excited about the new addition to our threesome. "You're going to have a little playmate soon," I cooed to Milo, who cocked his head as if to say, "You don't say!"

And so it was with great angst that I dialed Daryl's number, trying to ignore the gnawing in the pit of my stomach. The sound of her voice confirmed my fears.

"I'm sorry to inform you that I had to put Paris to sleep today," she said sadly.

I clutched my chest. "What?"

She explained that after Paris had gotten her shots, she'd not responded well. The vet diagnosed her as having some sort of neurological disorder.

I felt sick.

Daryl went on to say that she had another litter that would be ready in a month, but if I was too traumatized by the experience she would understand if I wanted my money back. However, she thought she had the perfect little girl for me—one with a lot of personality. She had planned to keep her for show, but since I was in the public eye she felt I should have a perfect-looking dog. Or perhaps I'd like to select another one from an upcoming litter?

I was numb. Before I knew it, I broke one of the sacred rules of dog selection. I mumbled something about how I would take the one she recommended and tried to focus enough to remember the date she would release my newly appointed charge into my care.

I hung up the phone and sat down. The import of what just happened descended on me slowly. I hadn't even absorbed the fact that once I picked up Paris she would be my dog for at least the next 14 years of my life, much less thought ahead to her impending mortality.

One day my dog would die. How would I bear it? Over the past four weeks I'd gotten used to the idea that I was going to own a dog and now Poof! she was gone just like that, only to be replaced by another dog I hadn't even seen. I felt stung. I hadn't even had a chance to fully bond with Paris yet. I didn't realize how much I'd really wanted her until she was gone. Amazing how many things we allow to slip away in life, not truly treasuring them until their absence magnifies their worth.

My friends felt it was a sign from God. "See! Perhaps God just wanted to see if you would be obedient. It was just a test. Take your 'out' while you still have it!"

But I dug in my heels. "Nope. I have to yield to this life lesson. I'm getting the dog, so get over it."

"Okay," they sighed, "but don't say we didn't warn you." Another friend teased, "Only you would get a brain-damaged dog."

It was the middle of a beautiful summer day when I finally picked up my new baby. With a little carrier on the front seat beside me, I set off, winding up the highway to Highland Park, finally pulling up in the tree-lined driveway. The dogs barked as Daryl ushered me in. Leading me back to the same bedroom where I'd first laid eyes on Paris, there sat the most beautiful little fluffy mound of toffee and white fur about the size of my hand I'd ever seen. She was my Milo! Her look said, "What took you so long?"

I was in love at first sight. Reverently I took her in my arms, and she cuddled close, smelling me to check me out. Then she nestled into the crook of my elbow just like she was used to being there. I handed over

the last payment installment to Daryl and proceeded to the car with my treasure. After settling Milan (the name I decided on after much deliberation with my friends—I chose another city I enjoy in honor of Paris) into her kennel beside me and getting a list of the right food and treats to get for her, we set off in search of a pet store.

Milan studied me as I drove. It was hard to keep my eyes on the road. I couldn't believe I had a dog, and she was so beautiful. We stopped at a pet store. I scooped her up, proudly carrying her into the store in search of food. Don't ask me why I waited until that day to get dog food. Perhaps I'd been too busy purchasing a crate, playpen, toys, and how-to books on crate training, raising puppies, how monks raise dogs—you name it, I bought it. I devoured every word, taking copious notes and repeating what I learned to my friends (who couldn't have cared less). But I let their teasing roll off my back. I was so focused. I was so ready for this puppy! That first day in the pet store with Milan I experienced my first moment of proud ownership. Yes, I had morphed into Annette, enjoying the adoration as everyone in the store cooed over my baby girl. And Milan was totally up for it, accepting admiration as if she were a rock star.

Finally, after arriving home and being welcomed by the doorman and everyone that I could make pay attention, Milan got the opportunity to check out her new digs. She went on a sniffing tour until she started sniffing in a circle. I scooped her up and put her in her pen. She looked at me, calmly relaying, "I'm cool with this."

And there we sat, appraising one another for the rest of the evening. My friends were all calling to see if I had indeed brought my little baby home. I was already sounding like a proud mother, telling them how gorgeous she was. Naturally I pulled out my camera and took way too many photos. Milan humored me until she yawned, suggesting she'd had quite enough of being on display.

As she settled into bed for the night, I was prepared to stay up all night with a whining, crying puppy because that's what everyone had warned. "Oh, she's going to cry all night. Get ready. The first few nights pups are separated from their mothers, they're up all night."

Not this one. She gave me one last glance, curled up, and went to sleep. Right before I went to bed I woke her up, put her on a Piddle Pad, she did her business, and then girlfriend was out like a light until morning. As I took one last look at her sleeping in her pen on the floor at the foot of my bed, I thought, *If I had known it was going to be this easy, I would have done this sooner.*

❧ Paws to Reflect ❧

Sometimes we don't know what we're missing. And the only thing separating us from joy is a simple decision. The reason most of us refuse to make decisions is because we're so busy thinking about what our decision will cost us that we forget to consider what will be gained. Usually what we gain will exceed the cost! But we often don't find that out until we take the leap of faith. Others can tell us about their fantastic experiences, but like snowflakes, no two experiences are exactly alike. Someone else's experience can't predict our own or what impressions will be carved in our lives by the occurrences and people we encounter.

Once we stop looking through the window of unknowing and decide to enter into the fullness of discovery, it's inevitable that we'll be richer for the knowing.

6

The Work of Forgiveness

Okay, if you're eating right now…stop reading. Come back later when you've finished your food.

This chapter is about the more unseemly aspects of dog ownership—namely their daily need to eliminate waste. Call this the poop and piddle chapter, if you want.

My friends warned me about this problem (and one of them even gave me a pooper scooper), but I didn't allow it to sink in. And though my dog ownership saga began because of this natural bodily function common to all canines happening in my building, I never thought about it in relationship to *my* dog.

Dogs piddle and poo. This is fact. Big dogs, little dogs, male and female—they all deposit little ponds, flowing rivers, tiny pellets, or surprising mounds of waste.

For the "pond" problem I quickly discovered the magic of the Piddle Pad. What an invention! This was totally going to make my life so much easier. Living in Chicago, one has to be cognizant that even though it is paradise in the summer, it can feel like freezing punishment in the winter.

No, Chicago is not the best of spots from mid January to March. I don't go outside unless I have to. And whenever possible, I go straight into my garage, get into my car, drive to my destination, find a spot as close to the door as possible, and then, later, return home to the safety of my condo.

Getting a dog was not going to change my winter routine...thus my celebration over the magical Piddle Pad. On days when the weather was unbearable, my dog wouldn't have to go outside. Milan would simply go to her piddle station. I loved this idea. And so the training began, and the piddle problem was no more.

But I never stopped to think about the poo factor.

When I first announced I was getting a shih tzu, my brother Ian chortled, "Do you know they eat their own stools?" He then dissolved into laughter, thinking this was very funny.

I was totally grossed out.

"Eww! I don't believe you," I said.

"You'll see," he replied with a devilish smile.

At first, all went well. When Milan pooed I picked up the Piddle Pad and flushed the poo down the toilet. However one day I didn't remove her handiwork fast enough, and I caught her mid nibble!

"No, no, no!" I waved her away frantically, causing her to look rather confused, like "What is the big deal, lady?"

Later a friend told me this was learned behavior. As newborn pups, they see their mother eating their droppings to keep the area clean and assume this is the thing to do. Someone else told me that dog poo contains nutrients, and that's why they do it. Whatever the reason, I thought it was gross! I certainly wasn't touching it, and I didn't see why she would want to either.

Eventually I ventured outside with Milan to the real world where everyone in the neighborhood was walking their dogs. I watched the great care and patience people exercised while waiting for their charges to sniff out the perfect spot for relieving themselves. After they had done so, their dutiful owners would bend and scoop up their offerings in little plastic bags, as if picking a flower to take home. After all, it was just part and parcel of having a bundle of love in your life. No big deal. So I too joined the throng of those joyfully picking up poo in handy little plastic bags without another thought.

What I quickly learned is that no one's dog is *just* his or her dog. Dogs are children—and don't you forget it! Just as if you have a baby and have to clean up behind him or her, it is no different with a dog. It's like changing a messy diaper. You just hold your nose or your breath and do it. Now that's love. Yes, though some may do it out of duty, fearing being fined by the city for not cleaning up after their pet, for most I think cleaning up after pets is done as a labor of love. A second-nature kind of thing that animal lovers don't think about.

Oh, the things we do for love!

Paws to Reflect

Perhaps this is also why a woman stays with a bad man for far too long, putting up with his mess and making excuses for him. Or why a mother clings to hope for the child she continues to love through foul up after endless foul up. Maybe it's also why God remains patient with us after we create messes again and again. I don't know about you, but I sure make a mess of things from time to time. I need only look back at my life and some of the stupid choices I've made to get a picture of God sitting on His throne shaking His head and thinking, *Look at that child! When will she ever learn? Oh well, here's another mess I'm going to clean up.* And He does just that time and time again. This reminds me of the song "If Not for Grace." I can so relate to the writer's musing on where he would be without the grace of God. He concludes he would be nothing more than a hopeless case, an empty space. Again I say I would just be a hot mess!

Sometimes we expect from people what we can only hope for and get from God. I attract lots of broken people in my life because I'm the sort who loves to nurture the wounded. But there's a point where my grace runs out and my patience is depleted. I don't beat myself up about it because I understand this is a part of my humanity that may get better in time, but then again, may not. It depends on my willingness to yield to God's surgical knife...and some days I'm not all that willing.

I'm being real here. My readiness to surrender varies. When I'm hopelessly devoted to God, I'm willing to do anything He asks. But on days when my devotion wavers, I'm off to the races in the opposite direction after whatever is winning my attention and affections. And yet God still loves me, puts up with me…and cleans up my messes when I repent and turn back to Him.

I can't say that about myself when it comes to people in my life who have pushed me beyond my limit. At some point my patience is gone and I want them to shape up and fly right. Sometimes I lose it. I want to hold their noses to the floor and insist they smell the messes they've made of their lives (and mine in some cases). Sometimes I'm not very forgiving. And definitely not as forgiving as God is toward me. But then again, I'm not as deeply invested in others as He is.

I realized, after some time, that those who were guilty of allowing their dogs to go in the hallway of my building had been renters. They didn't care about the condition of the building because they weren't invested in it. The owners were more careful because they knew their long-term investment was at stake. I realize that Satan, the enemy of our souls, is just like a renter. He tempts us to mess up, and after we do he rubs our noses in it and accuses us until we find ourselves buried beneath our shame. But God, who is eternally invested in us, simply invites us to acknowledge our mess and then graciously cleans it away, restoring our value. However, even though we've been forgiven, the stain or the consequence of our actions sometimes remains.

When I caught Milan having an accident in the middle of my living room floor, I wordlessly cleaned it up, knowing I had to punish her so she wouldn't do it again. I was surprised, though, that I wasn't angry at her. Milan's down time in her pen was more for her than for me. I didn't mind cleaning up after her. I just didn't want anyone else to have to do so. Let's face it, no one else is as invested in her as I am; therefore, they would never be as patient. I now understand parents who patiently suffer through the public tantrums of their child while everyone else around them rolls their eyes.

No one is really interested in cleaning up a mess they're not personally responsible for. At one point I stopped and pondered why I could be so longsuffering with Milan and so impatient with the people in my life. That's when it hit me. I had no great expectations of Milan being brilliant and getting it right every time. She is just a dog. So when some person I know does something I don't like or that I think isn't the best choice, why can't I just say, "She's only human," chalk it up to her humanity, and extend grace? Why do I expect perfection? The only flawless person who makes no mistakes is God! Oy vey!

From time to time when God doesn't do what I want Him to do, I confess I question His intentions and motives. I get impatient with Him too. I rant and rail and ask Him when is He going to show up. Sometimes I'm yelling so loud I can't hear Him say, "Michelle, I'm already here. I'm patiently waiting for you to get over yourself and own the mess you've made so we can clean it up together and move on." Lord, have mercy! And He does.

Now if I could only translate that live-and-let-live attitude beyond my dogs to people, I would be the most gracious individual on the planet. I'm getting there, bit by bit, poo bag by poo bag.

Perhaps that's why some of us struggle with bitterness and unforgiveness. Holding on to things that smell can affect you negatively and repel others. Picking up after others and dealing with their messes is very humbling. Being willing to throw the waste away without commenting on the smell is even more humbling. And yet when others forgive us or cover up our messes—*that* is even more humbling.

To be aware of our mess and know someone else saw it, bent over to deal with it, and didn't magnify it can increase our shame because in that moment we realize how undeserving of mercy we really are. That, my friend, is the true beauty of grace. Not the kind we say before a meal but the kind that scoops up your stuff in a little plastic bag and flings it out of sight without even a comment on the smell or the nature of it. The kind of grace that God is talking about when He sends out the invitation to come and reason with Him no matter how bad we've been, no matter how deep the stain of our sin. He's willing to wash us, make us clean, and fling our sins so far out of sight they'll be remembered no more. That is forgiveness at its best! Perhaps that's why it's so hard for us to practice forgiveness? It requires bending down and handling things that aren't pleasant.

Ah, but God does this all the time.

SoundBite
Breaking the Cycle

One fine morning I was out taking my usual stroll with Matisse and Milan. Matisse was anxiously pulling me toward the doggie park, getting more and more excited with every step. But I knew if we entered I'd be delayed getting back to the office so I chose to take the route around the doggie park and allow Matisse to sidle along the fence to say hello to one of his friends. As Matisse leaned in to sniff Cooper, a rather cute wheaton terrier, Cooper lifted his leg and relieved himself all over Matisse. As his owner tried to yank him away, Matisse just looked at Cooper, shook it off, and kept on moving. It didn't faze him one bit.

When someone rains on my parade (yes, that's a nice way to put it), I don't shake it off so easily. I don't care how many wonderful emails I get telling me how my books and messages have changed lives, it's the one mean, critical, and sometimes downright insulting one that stings long after I've read it. I writhe, I moan, I commiserate over what was said, questioning my abilities until someone makes me snap out of it. Though I try to shake it off, the criticism lingers like putrid perfume burning my nostrils and spoiling the air around me. And here was Matisse taking it all in stride, with no sign of an impending complex in sight.

Later that day the full impact of this interaction played out. When we went out for another walk I noticed that several dogs would sniff Matisse and then raise their leg to pee on him. I pulled him away laughing. Although I'd toweled Matisse off, I realized that the smell of Cooper's early morning baptism lingered and was now inviting others to follow suit. Off we went to take a bath before things got out of hand.

When the scent of rejection, pain, or disappointment buffets our hearts and is allowed to settle into our minds, it lingers and invites more of the same. Sometimes we don't even realize when the cycle started. We can't find our way back to the original moment that impacted all our tomorrows, but the scent of our despair follows us, setting us up to sabotage ourselves again and again. With each recurrence we become convinced that our greatest fears are true after all.

Once the sting of a setback has set in it's hard to shake. The reassurances of friends sometimes aren't enough to bring the restoration we need to move forward again. Our eyes become clouded by what we've experienced, and we lose our way, focusing on our failure instead of the next chance to get it right. The danger is that we too often follow what we focus on…so we lead ourselves to yet another broken place, never able to recover our equilibrium, never able to shake the smell of our pain on our own.

Yet all the while God waits, ready to wash us, to saturate us with His goodness. He's ready to restore our faith and hope for greater tomorrows and bathe us in more love than we've ever known.

As Matisse leaned into my hands and the fresh scent of Le Pooch shampoo wafted around us I thought, *How difficult we make it to free ourselves. How often we run from a good cleansing, maybe even denying our foul odor, refusing to believe we've sunk to such a level of unbelief that we believe life is stuck.*

We find it easier to allow others to dump on us, even though we don't like it. If only we could learn to shake it off. And when the stench of our experiences invites repeat offenses, if only we will submit ourselves to the hands of the One who can and will remove the stain of our suffering. He restores and heals us! A clear conscience and unfettered heart is a rich perfume that attracts endless blessings.

7

The Importance of Obedience

Before picking Milan up from Daryl, I not only read many manuals on how to raise the perfect dog, but I researched the best doggie schools in my area for Milan. I finally decided on Good Dog. They had a stellar reputation for teaching obedience with a gentle method. Oprah sent her dogs there, and...well, that settled it in my mind!

So I set up an interview appointment with Marilyn and Howard, the owners, to see if Milan would be accepted at Good Dog. Has she had her shots? Yes, she has. How old is she? Twelve weeks old. I answered all their questions and was happy when they told me Milan was admitted into their obedience program.

They told me, however, that it wasn't really Milan who needed to be trained—it was me. Owners are the source of most dogs' problems, they said, allowing their dogs to run amuck and then wondering why they are out of control later. *Kind of like parents,* I thought.

I would also have to attend a lesson once a week so I wouldn't undo Milan's training. They suggested I bring her in the day after I brought her home lest she settle into bad habits. They warned me to resist falling prey to her cute fluffiness, and they instructed me to limit her freedom until she earned it.

This was hard. Limiting Milan's freedom meant keeping her in her crate. It seemed so cruel. She sat watching me with those huge brown eyes that looked as if they had been enhanced with eyeliner.

She fluttered her two-inch eyelashes at me through the grill of the door. I felt like I'd put her into jail. I called Marilyn to see if I could relent, but she remained firm. "Dogs are den animals. She's fine. It makes her feel safe. She's not a person; she's a dog." I wasn't convinced of this, but I went along with the program.

Every day off to school we dutifully went. I dropped her off at nine and picked her up at five. Milan settled into her routine rather nicely, actually getting excited when we approached the school and she saw her teachers. She responded to their commands and eventually mine with the obedience of a first-born seeking to please. I was completely fascinated with how quickly she understood words and acquiesced to my instructions. It was a powerful feeling.

"Milan, sit."

And she would sit.

"Milan, come."

And she really would come right to me and then sit dutifully waiting for the next command. Wow! Every mother on the face of the earth probably wishes her child would do that! Nice pipe dream.

🐾 Paws to Reflect 🐾

Like humans, dogs have free will. But by receiving a reward when they obey, they strive to please every time because the thing they seek most is praise and love.

People are similar. No matter how much employees love what they do, and even though they get a check for what they do, they still crave acknowledgment, praise, and appreciation from their employer...or it takes the fun right out of what they're doing. The same can be said for a husband or a wife. I recall hearing a husband respond to the complaint that his wife voiced about the fact that he never told her she looked nice or enjoyed a meal she prepared. He said, "No news is good news." Well, not exactly. We're wired to desire praise and significance. We all want to know we're appreciated, that we did something well and someone we want to please has noticed. Milan lived for me to say "Good girl!" and give her a treat. The sun rose and set by my praise for her.

Perhaps this is why we sometimes get confused when God doesn't seem to acknowledge or respond to what we consider our "goodness." A spirit of entitlement seeps into our thinking. If we're doing all the right things and being good Christians, God should reward us with treats and a pat on the head…or give us a fabulous life free of trouble. When life happens around us, we run for cover, wondering what we did wrong or why God doesn't love us. Or we ask, "If God is so good, why does He let all of this awful stuff happen in the world? Actually, forget the *world*. Why does He let anything bad happen to *me?*"

Yes, we think God owes us something for our chaste behavior. And when we don't get a reward right away, we imagine Him to be an oversized bully punishing us unmercifully. Nothing could be further from the truth! Our bad choices do a good enough job of punishing us, which is why God tells us not to do certain things in the first place. He hopes we will love and trust Him enough to follow His directives because of all He's already done for us. Our obedience is our way of saying thanks to Him for loving and taking care of us.

This became crystal clear as I thought of my relationship with Milan. Milan owed me her obedience because of all the nice things I did for her. I provided a beautiful home, lots of toys, a wonderful bed, good food, and great care. She owed me. Being good was the least she could do. Now, I will say because she was so good I wanted to give her extra comforts and treats. But can you imagine if she had given me a "You owe me" attitude? I probably would have ignored her on purpose to humble her.

Respect and honor need to be earned, and God has more than done that for us. It's that terrible little thing called free will that gets us in trouble. We think just because we have it we should exercise it. You see, none of us really *has* to do anything God tells us to do. And some of us take that quite literally as we interpret the ten commandments as the ten suggestions.

This attitude causes us to miss out on a whole lot of treats. I've come to understand that God is not a cosmic killjoy sitting up in heaven thinking up ways to ruin our fun. His commands are for our safety. And to further entice us to be obedient, He attaches a blessing or treat to many commands and instructions. God says, "Honor your father and your mother." The treat? Things will go well with us and we'll have a long life (see Exodus 20:12). Sounds good to me. Perhaps this is why God says, "Give ear and come to me; hear me, that your soul may live" (Isaiah 55:3). It's not about Him being on some spiritual ego trip. After all, He is still God whether we come to Him or not. He wants us to obey Him for our own good.

My saying "come" to Milan is not about my exercising power over her, spoiling her fun, or robbing her of her independence. It's about teaching her to listen to my voice because my voice will keep her safe from danger. The command "come" could save her life in a situation where her distance from me threatens her well being. Drawing close to me gives her the advantage of my protection from an aggressive dog, a car, or a mean person. The closer she is to me, the safer she is.

Sometimes, just like Milan, I don't even realize when I'm in trouble. I'm skipping down the garden path enjoying the scenery and get blindsided by someone who doesn't have good intentions toward me. Or maybe it's just life in general with its mixed bag of unexpected inconveniences and tragedies. In these times I need to feel God's nearness more than ever. I know that if He is near, everything is going to be all right. And faithfully He is always near.

I remember as a child thinking my mother had eyes in the back of her head that were removable and mobile. I just knew her eyes followed me to school or wherever I was because she always knew what happened before I got home. It drove me crazy. And yet it was her watchfulness that made me line up and do as she said, even when peer pressure enticed me to sneak off and go against her will. After a while I learned that her way was the best way, and in most instances it was also the *safe* way, the way that led to a good life. And that was the treat.

At work when I did what my employer asked me to do, I got a

check. And if I was really good consistently, I got a raise and a promotion. How far I excelled was in proportion to the way I chose to honor my employer and do my job.

When I look at obedience in this light it's no longer something that robs me of my independence and power. It increases them. I'm put on the path to receiving everything I've ever wanted out of my relationships, out of my career, out of life. Rebellion and disregard for authority has cost me time and time again more than I want to pay. Lack of obedience to God is very costly. The brief exhilaration I experience from doing things my way is short lived, and the pain of the consequences of my willful choice lasts a lot longer than the pleasure in most instances.

My frustration when Milan decides to be stubborn and not come when I call is not just embarrassing at times, it's downright disappointing and causes me to worry. One instance of disobedience can cost her dearly or, worse, be a matter of life or death. I might be calling her out of harm's way or because I want to love on her, give her a treat, or rub her tummy. She will never know unless she comes. And if she chooses not to come, she could miss a blessing or incur a painful consequence for disobedience.

I suspect this is something God knows about us too...but still He doesn't insist on us doing what He says. We do, after all, have that sometimes dangerous free will. Can you picture God poised to give us treats—good health, abundance, joy, peace—all the good stuff we all want? I can! And yet we let Him down every time we refuse to come, refuse to sit at His feet and experience the love He so deeply wants to give us.

My friend Bill told me I shouldn't allow anyone else to feed Milan because only by total dependence on me will I gain her total love and obedience. Perhaps this is why we have such a hard time with God and obedience. We rely on so many other sources to feed us, love us, and validate us that our full dependence on God just isn't there. We eat from so many other hands that we fail to see why God should have our total devotion. And yet at the end of the day He is the source of everything we crave. Sadly, we miss the difference between being full and being satisfied when we're not focused on Him.

In the end, only what God gives can truly nourish and sustain us. We need to get past all the comparisons and totally trust Him. That doesn't make God a crutch, just someone who can ultimately make this journey we call life a lot easier. And that's a good reason to stop chasing deceptive bones and simply "come" when He calls.

8

The Interesting Thing About Expectations

Though I had given in to getting Milan, training Milan, looking after her, and picking up her poop, I did have my limits. One of those limits? *There will be no dogs on my bed!* Shouldn't something remain sacred? I wanted a *husband* in my bed, not a dog. And Milan was quite pleased to sleep on her favorite teddy bear on the floor at the foot of my bed...until one fateful day.

It was a gorgeous sunny day and I decided we should walk from my apartment all the way down to the shopping district, about a half hour away. We'd stroll through the shops a while and then meander back home.

Off we went, enjoying our leisurely tour of all things beautiful, stopping for moments of admiration along the way. We stopped at our favorite puppy boutique, Tails in the City, and visited with all the other puppies and puppy parents (notice I didn't call them owners) before continuing our jaunt.

After shopping, we headed home. By the time we were close to home, Milan was one tuckered little puppy. To make this perfectly clear she stopped and lay down on the sidewalk, refusing to go one more step. I picked her up, tucked her in the crook of my elbow, and continued. By the time I reached the building I was in total sympathy with how she felt. Retiring to the den I lay down on the couch to take a nap. Milan curled up on the floor next to me. When I looked down at her she looked so cute all snuggled up that a moment of tenderness flooded my heart. I scooped her up, placed her on my chest, and we both drifted off to Slumberland. I thought nothing of it until later that evening at bedtime.

I climbed into bed and got comfortable on my pillows, settling down for a good night's sleep when I became aware that I was being watched. Sure enough, as I looked down, there sat Milan studying me intently. As I looked in her direction she came closer to the bed until she was right next to it. She looked up at me with an air of expectancy.

"No," I said.

She cocked her head to the side as if to ask, "Why not?" And then she offered a very husky "Arf!" in an obvious attempt to question me.

"No!" I said and rolled over on my back to ignore her. My bed was off limits.

But Miss Milan was not to be deterred. Obviously she liked what she'd experienced during our afternoon nap. If she was good enough to sleep next to my heart on the couch in the den, why shouldn't she be good enough for the bed? With that rationale ingrained in her little puppy brain, she backed away from the bed, stopping when she was some distance away.

She sat and studied me for a moment, first looking at me, then cocking her head to the other side and looking the bed up and down, as if measuring the distance between the top of the bed and the floor. In a sudden burst she ran toward my bed at top speed. After gaining momentum and at just the right time, she bounded up toward the bed. I have one of those princess-and-the-pea mile-high beds, so she fell short of her mark and whacked the side of the bed. She fell back against the floor where, after sitting up and regaining some dignity, she barked in frustration. And let me tell you, she was not amused! I was, however. I couldn't stop laughing. I was beginning to discover Milan's intelligence. She was beautiful, prissy, and smart as a whip. What a princess! She had the nerve to have an attitude because she couldn't scale the bed.

Needless to say, my resistance quickly deteriorated and she was soon nestled next to me on a pillow fast asleep. That is until Milan woke up and tested her ability to get off the bed on her own. The bed was too high. I raised that if she had to piddle in the middle of the night she wouldn't be able to get to her Piddle Pad. So we came to an agreement. She would sleep next to the bed at night on her own bed and have cuddle time on my bed in the morning when we woke up.

🐾 Paws to Reflect 🐾

This experience taught me early not to start things I couldn't finish. And not to make promises I wouldn't be able to keep. I shouldn't commit to things I don't want to abide by long term. This way I'd avoid what messes up a lot of relationships.

Many a courtship starts off full throttle with both parties doing all sorts of romantic gymnastics to win the other person's love. Later the pursuit diminishes, opening the door to questions, suspicions, and dissatisfaction. The man who used to call every morning, noon, and night relaxes after he knows he's won the object of his pursuit. Now his woman is asking, "How come you don't call me the way you used to?" She doesn't understand the disruption in his pattern, and it causes problems and doubts.

Patterns are important. As human beings we rely on consistency as a compass to keep our relationships on course. The tension and release of knowing what to anticipate from the other person keeps us moving forward in our exchanges with one another because we build a comfort level of knowing there will be no monumental surprises. No one wants to be blindsided by things they're not ready for.

Expectations creep into every relationship. How we respond or don't respond to those expectations bears lasting consequences. The violation of expectations affects our ability to trust, which affects our ability to love and submit to each other. Expectations war with the concept of true love because love believes all things, hopes all things, endures all things.

Milan taught me about this in an entirely different light. Her trust in me—that I would do the right thing—got me to comply to her wishes. She didn't skulk away after I refused her entry to my bed. She persisted in pursuing her desire—a place near me. In the end she got what she wanted because she never thought I would turn her away. This was obvious in her refusal to go away once her own attempt to have her way failed.

And like the typical person, once she got her way the value of her acquired position diminished, and she could take or leave it. That's a whole other lesson isn't it? Sometimes what we want is much more appealing when it is out of reach. Take that dadburn piece of fruit Eve had to have that fateful afternoon in history that cost the world so much pertaining to eternity until Jesus rescued us. I've often wondered how tasty that fruit was after she bit into it. Was it as juicy and sweet as all the others she'd previously eaten with full permission from God? Or did she think to herself after handing it off to Adam, *Humph! I don't know what the big deal is. It isn't all of that. I could have saved myself the calories.* Who knows? But this was the beginning of wanting what we can't have—plotting, planning, and pursuing the gold ring only to be shocked that it's not really gold after we grab hold of it.

Faith makes me wait on God more patiently these days. The faith that not only does He want me to enjoy good things but also that He knows when it's the right time to indulge me. When I've submitted to His decisions about my life without questioning I can then sit lovingly in His presence without looking over His shoulder to see if what I want is coming. But at times, when I've finally exhausted myself trying to have my way on my own, when I've come to the end of my ability to leap the hurdles of life, I simply turn to Him and sit and wait too. That's when I feel Him pull me close to Him. As I press into enjoying Him, smelling the essence of His tenderness, listening to His heartbeat, and resting against Him I find that all the things I was jumping up and down about don't hold as much joy and peace as this. That's when I finally relax. In that moment God reaches into His robe and surprises me from within the folds of His garments with the things I want. I then respond with gratitude. No longer desperate for what I thought I wanted, I take what He offers without grabbing, holding it lightly, not feeling the need to possessively clutch it. Now I own it; it doesn't own me. And I'm glad He made me wait until I got to this place where I enjoy Him more than what I thought I had to have. It's all in perspective now. And hopefully more and more I'm turning to Him first...instead of going out on my own and being frustrated and disappointed.

Now sometimes on an evening when Milan has missed me more than usual, she decides to grace me with her presence and stay on top of the bed all night, snoring contentedly like an old man. And at these precious times I'm sure she thinks to herself after settling into the fluffy folds of my duvet, *Life doesn't get any better than this.*

And truly it doesn't when we've made peace with what we want, what we think we need, and found the truth of what really makes us happy. When we finally figure out that our best victories are the battles we win without insisting other people live up to our expectations, and we turn our attention toward wanting *them* more than what they can give. When we patiently wait for them to meet us at a common place of wanting, life gets good. So good you'll be surprised to find how little it takes to satisfy the soul.

9

The Flattery of Reflection

I quickly discovered the truth that dogs do take after their owners... or is it the other way around? I can't really say who is rubbing off on whom, but suffice it to say that I appreciate the fact that Milan is, like me, somewhat of a diva (in a good way, of course!). For instance, like me, Milan likes to sleep in. This is, by the way, a great relief! One of the things that caused me great worry about owning a dog was wondering, *Will I have to be up at seven every morning attending to the demands of my dog?* That *would just not work! I am* not *a morning person*. Rising at the crack of dawn would have been a sure deal breaker for me. Our romance would've been short-lived. So imagine my pleasure to find that Milan is even more vehement about not rising to greet the sun than I am.

I didn't realize how much of a morning dog she was not until Milo, Milan's little boyfriend from four floors down, spent the night with us. Annette, his owner...excuse me—his *mommy*—had to travel overnight and left him with me for a sleepover. Before she left Annette reminded me that Milo wasn't Piddle-Pad trained and would have to be walked first thing in the morning to avoid an accident.

So the next morning at seven I struggled to convince myself to get up. Looking out the window didn't help. It was a gray, late-fall morning in Chicago. Dreary.

But it was either take Milo out or suffer the consequences on my carpet. So I forced myself up, took Milo and a reluctant Milan, and headed out the door. Once outside, the morning was even worse than I thought. It was more like winter. Milan and I both did a step back once we got outside, both of us balking at the cold. Milo, however, was quite enthused about taking an early morning stroll. Milan being the efficient woman she is, quickly set about doing her business so she could get this frigid walk over with. She figured if she was done she could go back inside.

Not so with Milo, who continued sauntering down the sidewalk being quite particular about the spot he would choose to relieve himself. This thoroughly annoyed Milan, who began straining against her leash to head toward home, when I wouldn't comply.

"Stop it, Milan," I said. "Milo hasn't done his business yet." Milan kept pulling at her leash. Finally I set my heels, hanging on for dear life. But she was not to be deterred from retreating back to the warmth. She stopped, reared back, and began to wiggle. At first I didn't know what she was doing but then it became clear as she succeeded in wriggling out of her collar and turning to go home without me!

Meanwhile Milo, oblivious to our impatience, was plodding on, still sniffing to find the just the right spot. I yanked him in mid-sniff and headed after Milan to keep her from getting beyond my reach. I scooped her up, struggling to balance her in one arm while still holding Milo's leash with the other. I certainly understood how Milan felt about the situation, but I also knew that enduring the cold was the preferable choice over cleaning up an accident in my house.

I learned an important lesson that day. If I had to take Milo out early in the morning, I would go without Milan. She was not amused by the cold or the hour and was quite put out with Milo for disturbing her morning. By the time we got back to the house, she definitely had developed an attitude with Milo. Totally ignoring his friendly sniffs she sauntered toward her favorite teddy bear, curled up, and was asleep and snoring in no time flat.

Yup, Milan was definitely a lot like me. Persnickety and particular about her comforts. She was all girl.

Like me, Milan also loves to eat. I joke about the fact that she's built like me, with a short torso. She struggles with her weight the same way I do and has what I call "junk in her trunk" (that would be a rather plush tush).

Like me, she also cares very little for arduous exercise. She doesn't like the cold or getting her feet wet or dirty. Doesn't like anyone invading her space uninvited. She likes being social, but only at her choosing. Gracious and loving, she gives totally of herself…and then she is done, totally spent, ready for solitary solace.

The flip side is she can be quite a snob…or at least be perceived that way as she retreats to a quiet, out of the way corner when she feels she has expended enough energy on someone. She likes her space. She chooses when she wants to be social.

Because I understand her quirks, I deal with them accordingly. Milan acquired a wonderful wardrobe of sweaters and coats to accommodate the variety of temperatures that could dampen her enthusiasm for taking a walk. Boots also became a necessity after one dramatic occurrence.

We'd gone to Cleveland to visit friends and found ourselves literally snowed in. To my horror I realized this would be Milan's first time actually walking on snow. This was the same dog who stood up on her hind legs, front paws extended like a child to be picked up, when she came to a curb that had too much water in the gutter, refusing to even attempt crossing the moat. I didn't know how she would react to snow, but we had to give it a go because she had gotten to the place where she would only piddle on her pad and no longer poo. She had by now developed a preference for pooing outside because she didn't like the smell. (See, I told you she was a diva!) Therefore she would hold it until I took her outside.

It was late in the day, and she hadn't had a chance to go yet. I feared she would explode if I didn't take her out, so I put on her coat and out we went. At first everything was going amazingly well. She minced over the snow, testing every step tentatively before planting her steps, but at least she was moving forward.

After a while the urgency to do her business caused her to hasten her step as she frantically sniffed for a spot. Quite confused because the snow had blanketed everything green, she circled and sniffed faster and faster. Finally whether from frustration or freezing paws I'll never know, she landed in a whimpering heap on her side shaking furiously as if having an epileptic fit. It scared me so badly I didn't know what to do at first. I picked her up and cuddled her inside my coat, trying to calm her. She heaved a deep sigh, stopped shaking, and settled into the lining of my coat like it was a haven from the storm. I had been totally manipulated, and both she and I knew it.

Back inside I kept waiting for her to go to her Piddle Pad, but she never went. When there had been no bowel action by the next day, I was wondering if she was constipated. Later, to my chagrin, I learned she had quietly pooed behind the couch away from prying eyes. She was far too private to have strangers watching her poo on her Piddle Pad, which was in plain view in a corner of the family room. Always the princess.

Since that day, be assured, she has acquired rain slickers, Ugg boots, and pink leather boots. She's so cute in her boots and trust me, she knows it! She actually changes her carriage, strutting as she heads straight for the first snowbank she sees.

Once I dressed her up in her pink boots and a matching pink crushed velvet coat and went to Bloomingdales. She insisted on perching in the middle of the aisle where she could be admired by all who passed by. Batting her long lashes she knew she was beautiful and enjoyed hearing everyone tell her so. Always the consummate hostess of attention, she is totally self aware. She knows what she likes, knows what she doesn't like, and knows where everything fits in her world.

Milan also has an extensive toy collection. Gifts from neighbors and friends, along with my own guilt offerings every time I have to travel without her. Her delight is taking them one by one out of the toy box and placing them in the middle of the bedroom floor until they have formed a small pile she can climb up and lie down on. When she isn't lying on top of them, she will play with them one by one, dispersing them all over the room. I then gather them back up and put them in the toy box. She sits and watches me putting them all away. Then an hour later each toy will be returned back to its previous spot on the bedroom floor. The *exact* spot, as if she had designated them all a permanent position and only she knew what purpose they served there.

I giggle and think of the silent war between Marta, my cleaning lady, and me. Whenever Marta comes to clean, she cleans and gets inspired. Inspired to change how I've arranged certain things in my home, that is. Certain articles on shelves, the placement of two chairs in my living room, and so forth.

At first I thought that perhaps she'd forgotten where the items belonged and just haphazardly put them back wherever; but no, she would always put them back in exactly the same spot she had assigned them, even after I put them back where I wanted them. I knew this was a war I couldn't win because Marta was so bonded to my home I would tease her by thanking her for allowing me to stay there. So every other week after she's gone I patiently rearrange everything back to my liking. Just like Milan does!

Milan is a mini me! All the way down to complaining about things under her breath when she isn't pleased, which she promptly stops when I ask her what her problem is. She sits and looks at me as if to say, "You know what's wrong. Don't pretend you don't." Which is exactly what I say in the same circumstances.

Yes, Milan is truly a reflection of me—the good, the bad, and the in-between.

Paws to Reflect

Walking down the street I often chuckle because a lot of people look like their dogs, and not just in physical appearance but behavior as well! It's quite fascinating once it hits you. There is no denying that dogs reflect those who love and nurture them. This can be good or bad. Crazy owner, crazy dog. Good owner, good dog. The physical similarities are more obvious and at times quite comical. Like the bald-headed guy down the street who bears an uncanny resemblance to his bulldog. Or the lady who looks like a real-life Barbie doll with her matching Maltese.

How narcissistic can we be as a society? Doesn't this cross over to the pride we feel when we look at miniature versions of ourselves as we gaze upon our children? Like father, like son. Like mother, like daughter. We like the sound of that—until our offspring do something bad. It would be nice if they only imitated our good behavior, but unfortunately the apple doesn't fall far from the tree.

I even think certain married couples who've become good friends over the years also begin looking more alike as the years roll by.

Could this be what God desires from us? That our relationship with Him be manifested in our behavior as we take on more and more of His attitudes and personality? So much so that we finally look like Him, become like Him—true imitators of Christ, which is what the word "Christian" actually means—"little Christs"?

In looking *to* Him we actually become more *like* Him. We begin to reflect His beauty and grace and love to others around us, causing them to draw close and love Him too.

Could it be that we begin to look like what we truly love? Perhaps this is why Jesus said, "If you love me, you will obey what I command." He knew loving obedience could never be achieved by rules or coercion. But love...ah... Love makes me draw close, melting into oneness with the object of my affection until more and more of myself is crowded out of the equation. I become consumed with the one I love. I mirror the one I am focused on, willingly becoming a reflection of him or her because it feels so good I don't mind losing the parts of me that stand in the way of becoming truly one with my beloved.

I want to look like God. I want so badly for people to see God when they look at me. To be reminded of Him through the things I say and do. Sometimes I have a really good day at pulling this off and sometimes I don't. That's when holiness looks like a mountain too high for me to climb.

And that's when I know I need to draw a little closer and love

God a little deeper. To look deeply into His eyes and mirror what He is saying and doing. Absorb how He is feeling until I have the same reactions to people and the things around me that He has. Becoming holy by second nature minus the stress to perform.

It will be like breathing without thinking. And I won't mind losing myself and looking like God because it feels so good. And that my friend, is a beautiful thing.

10

The Secret of Conversion

For more than 20 years three of my closest friends and I have been meeting regularly to celebrate our birthdays. It's become a tradition with deep and abiding significance for all of us. Every few months another birthday rolls around and plans are set in motion.

The gift wish list is gathered along with the birthday girl's desired menu. The remaining three girls divvy up assignments, and off we go to our individual tasks to create a special day for the guest of honor. When the big day arrives, we meet at my house. I will either cook the requested menu or we'll go to the restaurant of choice, and then come back to my house for dessert, the opening of presents, prayer, and a sleepover.

We've carefully guarded this tradition over the years. It was the club of "us four and no more" for years. Only two other people have been able to penetrate the club. I'm always being accused of violating the rules because I often have people staying at my house on the big day and want to include them in my social activities. This is how my two friends Valencia and Sheila wiggled their way into the festivities. Brenda, Michelle, and Theresa came to love them, but I was warned not to try this too often.

And then along came Milan. Milan was not just a sleepover houseguest, she was a permanent fixture. Brenda was apprehensive. Theresa couldn't wait to see her—she loves dogs. But Michelle, well, she was none too pleased about this new member to our prayer clutch. She didn't know if this was going to work...until she met Milan.

Ironically, although Theresa was the one who really liked dogs and owned a rather lovable boxer named Chopper, Milan chose to focus on Michelle, who didn't like dogs, and Brenda, who was undecided. Milan easily won Brenda over in a matter of minutes, and then turned her attention toward Michelle. My baby girl totally understands the concept that in order to have friends you must show yourself friendly. So Milan followed Michelle everywhere and even chose to lie at her feet while we talked. By the end of the evening she'd made her way into Michelle's arms. Michelle finally concluded, "Okay, let the record show I still don't like dogs…I only like *this* one."

Her reaction reminded me of the time one of my white friends told me I was "different" from other black people. I thought that was an interesting comment. In retrospect, the truth of the matter is the only difference between me and those other black people to which my friend was referring was that she knew me and she didn't know them. It's hard to love and accept what you don't know. Her comment wasn't really true. We're all basically the same. We have the same needs and desires—to be loved, healthy, whole, and comfortable in life.

Yes, we respond to things differently, based on our surroundings and influences, but that's really about it. However, observing others from afar can cause our imaginations to come to false conclusions about people we don't know. Our wrong assumptions can lead to unfounded fears and prejudices.

After the experience with Michelle, I decided that Milan had found her calling in life—converting those who didn't like dogs into dog lovers. I wondered if she overheard me quoting the scripture that "he who wins souls is wise" because she certainly is wise in that regard. She has an uncanny way of perceiving exactly how to win over those who are nervous, fearful, disdainful, and even allergic.

One day a nice lady from Nigeria came to visit. Upon learning I had a dog, she refused to come in. She'd had a bad experience with a dog and was deathly afraid of them. I assured her that Milan wouldn't bother her. I finally convinced her to come in from the hallway.

Milan sat in the foyer gazing at her with great concern. Assessing that this woman was afraid, Milan retreated from the hallway to allow our nervous guest in without incident. Once in, this Nigerian woman perched on a chair in the hallway feeling more at ease being close to the door where she could beat a hasty retreat should she need to do so. Milan sat across the room, head cocked to the side, studying her quietly. After a short stare she stretched out to take a nap deciding fear was not exciting enough to warrant any further energy or attention.

The lady was outdone. She turned to me and asked, "Is that all she's going to do?"

"Mmm hmm," I smiled. "She knows you're afraid so she won't bother you. She's quite well adjusted that way."

"Do you think she would let me pet her?" she said.

"Oh, I'm sure she would love that." I suppressed a laugh. Milan didn't move as my visitor slowly made her way toward her. My child just batted her eyelashes at her, weaving her usual magic. Just before the lady got to where she was, she rolled over on her back. I laughed out loud. "I forgot to tell you, she lives for a good tummy rub. You have now earned the chance to be her best friend."

Tentatively the lady bent down to rub Milan's tummy. And Milan let her, slowly rolling from side to side to indicate where she wanted to be rubbed next. I tiptoed away as the lady slid to the floor to sit and pet Milan.

An hour later when my guest was leaving, she turned to me and said, "I've never liked dogs, but if I ever do get a dog I want one just like that one." This is the chorus I hear time and time again as one by one Milan converts every visitor at my home. Those who had heard about her before they came to the house assumed what they heard from me was pure exaggeration. But after experiencing Milan for themselves they sound like the Queen of Sheba after a visit with King Solomon of Israel, "Truly the half had not been told!" Some go away with a different view of dogs, and others go off to get their own dogs. Some decide to adopt Milan because they are afraid that if they got a dog it wouldn't be like her. But all go away changed after their encounter.

Perhaps it's because Milan is secure in who she is and the fact that she is loved. Whatever it is, she is never pushy or insistent on gaining anyone's attention or affection. Fear bores her. When my nieces, Lauren and Erica, were younger they would come to visit and start screaming when Milan approached them at the door. Her response? To walk away as if to say, "Oh get a life!" She refused to take it personally. Her only interest is in getting a tummy rub, and if you can't supply that, well, what good are you? Eventually, after Lauren and Erica overcame their fear, Milan had a different problem. They wouldn't leave her alone! She resorted to finding a comfortable spot under the coffee table where they couldn't reach her. But only after using them to get a tummy rub. She is no dummy!

One of the teachers at Good Dog asked me one day, "When are you going to break the news to Milan that she's a dog?"

"Are you kidding me?" I replied. "I don't think she would receive that well." Nor would it make a difference. She is her own dog, except she is like a little person. Yes, that's it. All my friends came to the conclusion that she is really a little furry person who stole their hearts when they weren't looking.

Paws to Reflect

Just as God woos us with His love and grace, and people are changed through a relationship, the secret to winning friends and influencing people seems to be much more simple than we make it. Perhaps we spend too much time trying to strong arm others to our way of thinking. From politics to religion, emotions can run high, making us overly passionate, maybe sometimes even obnoxious zealots who turn people off more than convincing them to consider our thoughts on a matter. If people are too busy defending themselves, they can't really appreciate or consider our point of view, can they?

Milan never insists that anyone love her. She is just lovable. She doesn't try to push or rush my visitors' conversions. She simply is who she is while allowing my guests to be who they are. It's as if she understands that it needs to be their decision to embrace her. She can't force the issue or change their minds. She can only respond to their change of mind by reinforcing it positively.

Can we learn from her example? Yes! Perhaps I don't need to be so insistent when trying to get others to see things my way. In order to get people to understand, they have to be willing to stand under what you believe. No one wants to stand under people who are bullying them and beating them into submission. But when you walk with someone in relationship, not threatening, but just loving, they will champion you, embrace you, and in some ways be changed just because of your presence. It's not what we say, it's who we are that changes peoples opinions.

My brother had a pit bull that made me extremely nervous. He assured me they were not as mean as everyone made them out to be, that it was a matter of how they are trained. When I finally met Carmi I had to agree. She is so cuddly and affectionate. She acts like a lap dog. It totally changed my attitude about pit bulls. I understand that dogs and people alike are a product of their environment and nurturing. These are the things that transform our nature. And our nature affects others around us.

Though I may be passionate about what I believe, and it is a part of my nature to be adamant about things I hold dear, if I truly want this to translate well to others I have to be considerate of those I'm trying to win, just like Milan is. She never presses past the boundaries of others. She honors them and waits for them to open the door. Meanwhile she remains authentically herself in her own space.

Perhaps Christians don't need to scream that everyone needs to get saved. Perhaps we can make having a relationship with God look so good that those searching for peace and true joy will ask, "How do I get what you have?" Perhaps it's as simple as having such a rapturous love affair with Jesus that others get jealous of what we have and want in. This is a much more pleasant way of affecting people for Christ. Attraction versus the repulsion of pummeling them with our convictions. Kinda like when Eve took a bite out of that fruit, chewed it as if it were the most delicious thing she ever ate, and handed it to her husband. Adam didn't care what it cost; he had to have a bite too.

Perhaps we need to lighten up on our opinions and *live* what we believe about God, race, politics—you name it. Just *live it out in a way that makes it desirable* to those around us.

Maybe, just maybe, we should quietly live and love allowing the fruit of our lives to set inviting standards until someone asks us for what we have. Then we can freely and gently offer it.

And guess what? Then, and only then, will they be ready to receive it wholeheartedly.

SoundBite
What Real Love Looks Like

I had a date recently that reminded me why I don't date often. Things started out well enough, but by the end of the evening I wondered why I left the comfort of my home to come out and be annoyed. At the end of the date I knew it was a waste of my time, and I silently filed my escort at the very back of the "friend in case of need" file.

I won't even bother to go into the details. Suffice it to say I hate playing games, and I hate being tested. I just want to be me and be loved and accepted on that very basic premise. I don't want to have to work so hard for something that should be organic, at least in the beginning. That lousy date made me go home and appreciate even more the love I have there. One of my closest friends, Bill, has it right. He says, "Your dogs are the only creatures on earth you never have to question." They keep it real. They just love. No matter what I do or don't do, they love me unconditionally and without testing. Even when I've upset them love overrules how they feel. They're soon back again for another cuddle, forgiving without a backward glance. What a good illustration of what God means when He says He can only stay angry at us for a short time. He loves us too much to stay mad!

On those occasions when I've traveled too often and left Milan and Matisse at school too long, when I return they are a bit standoffish. Maybe they think making me feel I wasn't missed will make me feel bad about leaving them behind. And believe me it works. They accomplish their mission. But they can only hold out so long before they're bouncing back into my arms with boundless fervor. Seeing their behavior and experiencing their love helps me believe I can hold out for a man who is authentic and comfortable enough with himself to keep it real with me. No games. Milan and Matisse remind me what real love looks like and keep me from accepting bad behavior from those who don't love me. I agree with the authors of *He's Just Not That into You,* pets are God's way of saying, Don't lower the bar just because you're lonely. God says we should never compromise ourselves. So if you want to wake up next to someone that loves you, get a dog! They don't test you. Play mind games with you. Lie to you. Use you and leave you. They stay until the bitter end, loving you just as much, if not more than, the day before. They are faithful. They trust blindly, passionately, with all of their hearts, following wherever you lead without question. The same way we should be with God.

I wonder if sometimes God thinks we're bad dates…

11

The Pull of Passion

"Michelle, do you realize that when you leave Milan waits for you by the door until you come back home?" my mother asked.

I had no idea! My mother went on to tell me that she tried calling Milan to play with her when I went out, but my dog wouldn't be distracted from her mission—waiting for my return. She parked herself on the rug in front of the door and waited patiently until I came home. It never occurred to me that this was what she did.

Since she never messed anything up, jumped up on furniture, or chewed on anything, I let her have full run of the house when I went out. On only one occasion, when I had exceeded my normal four-hour absence and she decided I had been gone too long, did she act out in a most uncharacteristic way. Well, maybe not so uncharacteristic. Shih tzus love to tear up paper.

On this particular day I was gone about six hours, carried away in a frenzy of dining out and shopping with a friend. Upon opening my front door it looked like I had entered a war zone. Paper was shredded and scattered all over the hallway and dining area. The neat stack of magazines I left in the hallway on the floor were obliterated like the ash that settles after a good fire.

"What did you do!" I scolded as I put my hand on my hip and looked down at Milan. She hung her head in contrition. "Shame on you!" This deepened her regret. It hurt my heart, but I knew I had to punish her. I scooped her up and put her in her pen, locking the door with a flourish lest she miss the significance of her actions.

I then walked away, leaving her to consider what her tantrum had cost her. She gazed through the bars of the pen looking most forlorn. I refused to look at her as I came and went for the next two hours. At one point I went into the bedroom, leaving her in the other room alone. She whined.

"Silence!" I ordered, and she obeyed.

After two hours I felt she'd suffered enough. It tortured her not to be able to be where I was, and she seemed especially outdone that I wouldn't even look at her. I opened the door and she slunk out of the pen, head hung down, groveling at my feet, begging for forgiveness. Truly she was sorry. I was convinced of that. Gently I picked her up and snuggled her. She heaved a grateful sigh and licked my face in apology. She's never touched another magazine or anything not offered to her to play with again, so she has re-earned the right to roam free.

And now I discovered she waited by the door for me. In my mind I imagined that while I was out Milan capriciously cavorted around the apartment enjoying her freedom. What a revelation!

I remember the times in college when I waited anxiously like a love-sick puppy for the young man I was enamored with. I would sit and stare at the phone, willing it to ring. And when it did I had to wait a beat so I wouldn't sound too anxious. That all went out the window the moment I heard his voice. I had gotten my fix. I could relax—for now. But when he didn't call as soon as I wanted the next time, my stomach would again grow queasy from the thought that he might not ever call again. I would die, I decided. I would just die if he didn't want me anymore. So if the phone rang and it was someone else on the line, I had a difficult time masking my disappointment. It was for him and him alone I waited. And so it was with Milan. No one else would do. It had to be me. I gotta love that!

I soon discovered that this longing for my presence went beyond simply waiting for me to return. Her devotion was greater than even that. I noticed that she would always wait to eat when I ate. I would set her food out, but if I didn't stop to eat she would ignore the offering. The moment I sat down to eat, she would sashay over to her bowl and devour whatever was in it.

One day I finished eating early and left the room before she finished her dinner. She stopped eating and followed me into the other room. It boggled my mind that she would rather be near me than finish her tasty meal. There she sat, looking up at me, wagging her tail in anticipation of a pet from me. This rocked me to my core. This type of devotion is too deep to comprehend.

I once attended a seminar where I learned that in order to change a habit we have to desire something else more than what we presently love to be able to turn away from the addictive habit. In that moment I knew Milan loved me more than anything (even food!), and it blew my mind. Let's face it. I know my mother loves me, and I know both my fathers love me. Sure my friends love me, and even my readers and admirers say they love me. But the question is, How much?

I learned quickly not to believe my own press through one majorly disappointing turnout at a conference I hosted. After tons of letters asking when I was going to have a conference of my own, I decided to have one. But after all the planning and advertising, the turnout wasn't what I expected. What happened to all the people who said they loved me and would come? I sure wasn't feeling the love as I pored over the bills I had to pay out of my own pocket because the attendance hadn't covered the cost. But then I had to reflect and adjust my attitude. It wasn't that my readers and fans didn't love me, it was just that they loved something else more—the time the weekend afforded them to do other things, prior commitments, the shoes they would rather buy over paying the registration fee, whatever. I couldn't take it personally. I had to accept that as beloved as I was, I was not a top priority when stacked against a list of other pressing needs and desires. Perhaps I'm not always the top priority with those I know and love, and neither should I expect to be. But I am Milan's greatest priority. Being in my presence is her foremost desire, and that warms my heart and makes me love her more.

🐾 Paws to Reflect 🐾

This brings to mind Jesus praying in the garden before He was betrayed. There has been a lot of thought about why He prayed for the cup of suffering to pass from Him.

Was He afraid?

I don't think so. After all He came to die. He never intended to stay. No, what He dreaded most was being separated from His father. He had never been separated from Him before, and Jesus knew that when He became sin for us He would be away from God's presence in that final moment of sacrifice. And that was an unbearable thought.

We were the leverage that compelled Jesus toward the cross. He weighed a brief separation from His Father against an eternity of separation from us, and His desire to have us be with Him won out. Wow! I don't know anyone else who loves me like that! How can I not love someone who loves me without reserve? It's impossible to resist pure love.

Many a man (and a woman) has fallen in love with someone he or she might never have considered except for the goodness or the love the person showed. Even I once got sucked into the charm, wit, and romantic advances of a man I normally would never have looked at twice. He carried me when I had injured myself. He buttered my bread and fed me in an exclusive restaurant. He told me I was beautiful and made me feel that way. I fell hard. Bang! I was in love. I was in love because he loved me.

By the same token, I love Milan because Milan loves me. I am her sun, her moon, her everything. It's that "love begets more love" thing. I wonder how much more I'd understand and see how God's heart swells over me if I loved Him like that. I mean *really* loved Him. Down to my very core. Where nothing else mattered but basking in His presence and pleasing Him—no matter what it cost me.

I know God loves us all. But does He have favorites? Even though

He's not a respecter of persons, treating us all fairly, I think perhaps He *does* have favorites. Many parents do. And I imagine parents also have children who at times drive them a little nuts. For instance, some kids just have a sense of entitlement that can turn off even the most loving parent. They kind of have the attitude that because you're their parents you should just do for them. Like it's an inescapable obligation no matter how much they disrespect and abuse you. Yeah, you love them all right, and you do what any good parent would do for them, but that's it.

Then there are the children who truly honor and respect you. They dote on you. They love you up without expectation of anything in return. Parents will have a hard time not wanting to reward such children by giving them what they want.

Since we're a reflection of our heavenly Father, I have to think we've inherited His heart attitude. Even God says He hates those who hate Him and loves those who love Him. So doesn't it stand to reason that those who love Him extra and nurture His heart get an extra portion of His affection and blessing? He's not pushing Himself on anyone who doesn't want Him, but He gladly responds to those who open themselves to Him. This is just my personal opinion, but it's definitely something to think about.

All I know is when I really think about how good God has been to me and my heart grows tender and I weep over the realization of it all, I can feel Him draw extra close. And the pleasure I feel in those moments is profound and deep. It feels so good I always wonder why it takes me so long to get there and why I don't do it more often. I *bask* in it. His nearness is sweet and palpable. And I am loathe to disturb the moment or tear myself away.

This is when I understand how Milan feels when she waits for me by the door. I finally get what it means to long for God's return when we will never be separated again. And the more I long for Him, the more of Himself He gives to me until I'm filled to overflowing with His goodness and His love.

To tell you the truth I don't *always* desire Him that intently, but I'm working on it. And I hope in those moments He feels about me the way I feel about Milan when I think of how much she loves me, even when my hunger for God's presence doesn't match Milan's desire for mine.

12

The Intrigue of Community

Once you get a dog, a whole new world opens up. Like *Star Trek,* it is truly a new frontier. I never realized the fastest way to make new friends was to get a dog. Who needs internet dating to meet guys when a pup will do?

People who never spoke to me before now stop and hold lengthy conversations, all because of Milan. And like any secret society, I never know who else has a dog until I mention Milan in a social setting. All of a sudden the energy in the room changes. Ears perk up. Excitement enters eyes. Smiles transform countenances. Stories begin to flow of the funny, silly, and heartwarming antics of our children.

You see, a dog is never just a dog to a true dog lover. That dog is a beloved child that never grows up. Yes, dogs may have their own maddening habits and mischievous antics, but at least they never go on drugs, bring bad friends home, or marry people who will break your heart.

I also quickly learned that pet lovers are gentler, kinder people. Scientifically it has been proven that animals can be very healing. They can positively affect blood pressure, stress levels, and heart health. *Pets are good for us!* They calm us. I'm a witness to that. When my hair is on fire over something that has upset me, one look at Milan brings my voice down several octaves. Because she's so sensitive to my moods, when she senses I'm upset she draws near with furrowed brow, looking quite concerned, ready to offer a quick touch that always distracts me from the issue that has me stressed out. A few snuggles later I'm calmer and able to focus on finding a solution.

My circle of friends has definitely widened since adopting Milan. Before Milan, walking down the street was a solitary experience. Now it's peppered with delightful encounters. You see, dogs are more social than people. They have their own social rituals that we humans will never understand—like their peculiar need to sniff one another's personal parts. At first it was embarrassing...until I learned that it's through their sense of smell they relate to one another. It's all about smells for them.

Actually this is also true for humans...only we call it chemistry. With us, our pheromones play a part in physical attraction, sometimes distracting us away from the things we really should be paying attention to. Far too often we couple up based on chemistry versus good sense. If we follow the scent of love, we tend to ignore or overlook other important signals. With dogs, sniffing is part of the dance, the meet and greet. The beginning of friendship. And so they sniff, sniff, sniff, settle how they feel about one another, and decide to play or not to play. And while they play, the parents talk.

I admit I seldom if ever remember the parents' names. Once I was out grocery shopping when this lady walked up to me and said hello. I said hello as if I knew her, but she sensed I didn't recognize her.

"I'm Molly's mom," she added.

"Ooh!" I exclaimed. Molly was the shih tzu with the long hair that lived in the building across from us. This was Hillary with a daughter in New York. Once the fuzzy connection was made, we went on to have a lengthy discussion about real estate in New York. She inquired about how Annette, Milo's "mom" (remember Milo was Milan's boyfriend), was doing since her move to New York. This led to a discussion about the inflated cost of owning a dog in Manhattan, as well as the perils and rigors of finding a new home there. After that encounter we became fast friends, and I even suggested a new hairdo for Molly.

Not only do you make a host of new friends who own dogs, but you also get to interact with a lot of admirers. Cute men, nice ladies, you name it—they all stop to pet your dog and ask questions. I also observed that dogs give lonely people an excuse to reach out to others. A dog is "safe" for people who fear rejection from people. Anyone seeking a respite from isolation is sure to get a friendly response either from the owner or the dog. Everyone's defenses are lowered, and the way is paved to exchange casual niceties that may or may not lead to anything in particular. Perhaps in some cases a pleasant experience is enough.

I recall going to a department store one day and encountering a lonely lady who asked if it was all right to pet Milan.

"Sure," I said.

The lady lowered herself to the floor, and the sight brought tears to my eyes. Milan must have sensed that this woman was really hurting because instead of her usual roll over in anticipation of a belly rub, she forsook her own selfish desires and snuggled up to the woman, resting her head on the woman's breast. As the lady bent to nuzzle her Milan licked her chin tenderly. I had taught her never to approach anyone's mouth, so she ever so gently loved on the stranger's cheeks and neck. I almost felt as though I was encroaching on a private moment. As the woman quietly wept, Milan continued to comfort her. I was speechless. Milan's threshold for being held doesn't exceed two minutes for the average person...unless Milan feels she is needed. And this day she felt very needed.

Finally the woman thanked me and rose from the floor. Milan sat looking up at her, as if to make sure she was going to be all right. My throat was tight so I just nodded. It was a moment of silently understanding unspoken pain. She seemed grateful that I asked no questions, but none were necessary. We parted. I was feeling pretty proud of Milan because she allowed herself to be used as an instrument of comfort. As we walked away Milan turned back to take one last look at the woman who had gone her own way. Then, as if being assured that she had done her part to extend healing, Milan sashayed down the sweater aisle with a new sense of purpose.

Another community many dog owners in large cities find themselves involved in is dog walkers. When parents are unable to break away from work to take their dogs on a potty run in the middle of the day, these are the men and women who save the day…or perhaps just the rug. There are also those who do their part to keep our dogs looking their best. John the groomer always imagines stray hairs where there are none. He is a perfectionist through and through, and I'm not mad at him for that. What Vidal Sassoon is to the precision cut, John is to dog grooming. Many pride themselves on being his clients, including me. But I find dog walkers the most intriguing, with groomers a close second.

Take Joanne. She loves animals. When I say Joanne loves animals I feel as if I should have another word for love that goes beyond the normal threshold of loving. Here is a woman who went to New Orleans after Hurricane Katrina to rescue dogs and cats. But it doesn't stop there. Oh no, she's been to Bosnia to rescue animals! Bosnia with sniper fire and all! Not exactly where someone would want to venture on purpose these days. Joanne's is not a casual love affair. She loves animals, and they love her back. Because, after all, animals sense when someone loves them, fears them, or hates them. Highly discerning and sensitive, they are your best alarm to determine if someone is not a good person.

You can tell a lot about a person by the way they respond to animals. It's been said that most people who are cruel to animals are cruel to humans as well. Many murderers have animal abuse somewhere in their histories. But in Joanne's case, by observing her with animals, you can tell she also is a people lover. Kind, considerate, and witty, she lights up the room with delightful conversation whenever I encounter her. She is one of the most caring people I know. I spent a Sunday afternoon sipping tea with her at one of the local hotels. She looked absolutely beautiful, and she delighted in being all woman minus her usual sweat and khaki dog walking outfit. We had a wonderful time chatting about her life experiences. She is truly one of the most interesting women I've ever met.

Then there was Tim, God rest his soul. He is now walking dogs in heaven. Tim was an art director for a top-level ad agency and decided he preferred the simpler life of communing with loving furry creatures instead of dealing with irate clients and crazy creative types. Chatty with a great sense of humor and a gentle nature, he was easy to love. Milan adored him. And there were others. All strolling the halls of the apartment building where I lived, as well as the streets surrounding the neighborhood from morning to late afternoon. They all knew one another—the gossip, the dramas, the neighborhood intrigues—and supported and covered one another. They were their own community. And now I was part of that. My life became filled with these loving, fun people. More people to love and be loved by. Life grows richer by the day!

Paws to Reflect

I'm reminded of a story in the book of Acts in the Bible, when Christianity first spread after the resurrection of Christ. Jews from everywhere had come to observe the Passover. That's right, the first Christians were Jewish. Jesus' disciples were all locked up in an upper room hiding out, still traumatized by His death, resurrection, and second departure when He ascended into the heavens before their eyes.

And now they were left waiting—for what they didn't know. But all of a sudden they were visited by and baptized with the Holy Spirit. They began to boldly proclaim the Good News of Jesus from the rooftop of where they were staying. Supernaturally their message was translated into every language represented in the crowds and thousands were converted. No one could understand how men (most were uneducated) learned to speak to them in their own language. But their connection was fused as they embraced the disciples' message. As their love for Christ became their common ground, they chose to share all things.

Talk about communal living at its finest! The early Christians pooled all their resources so that no one would be in need. No matter what the background, their language, status, or upbringing, none of the things that previously divided them did so any longer—all because of the one thing they now had in common: They all loved and were devoted to Jesus Christ. That powerful bond caused them to set aside all their natural differences. And that, my friend, is what love does. It unifies. It shatters walls. It tears down division. It wreaks havoc with isolation and forces us to engage in one big group hug no matter what.

I don't know if Annette, Milo's mom, and I would have ever noticed one another or become the close friends we are today if it weren't for that cute fuzzy little puppy named Milo. But a bond was forged the day we committed to babysit one another's dogs, have play dates, and walk them together.

And the more time our dogs spent together, the more time we spent together and now a deep friendship exists. Right before Annette moved to New York, she and Milo lived with me for three months. It was great fun having a multidog house, and when they left I felt their absence like a gaping hole. Annette had grown from a friend into a sister. We were a community, sharing all things in common—trials, space, meals, dogs, commentaries on our favorite television shows. As a single person it gave me a new perspective on the pleasures of sharing my life with someone. It pulled me outside my self-centeredness and made me a giver. And that is exactly what we were created for—life outside of ourselves. We are blessed not for hoarding but so we can be a blessing to others. I discovered that the more I do this the more enjoyable life becomes. The richer and fuller my days, the more satisfying and fulfilling existence is.

Who would have thunk that one small dog could open up a whole new way of living and loving? Pulling me beyond my little personal space without saying a word, simply by being and giving all she had to give, which is love.

At the end of the day that's all that is really expected of any of us—no more, no less.

13

The Trouble with Jealousy

Milan has a way with the boys that drives them to distraction. I decided to watch and learn. One thing I noticed was that although Milan was hot for Milo, she knew when to show her feelings...and when to withhold them.

Two examples illustrate this. First was how she behaved when we were on our way to his house. The first time we visited, she took off ahead of me when the elevator door opened. Then, sniffing her way down the hallway to his apartment she stopped at his front door and sat patiently, waiting for me to catch up. I'd forgotten the apartment number and wasn't sure this was the right door, but she knew where her man lived. I tentatively knocked, hoping she was right. There she sat wriggling and grumbling under her breath, voicing her impatience at why it was taking Annette so long to open the door. The moment Annette cracked the door Milan was through it in a flash. All was right with the world as she and Milo embraced one another in a dance of celebration at being together at last.

On another occasion Milan knew the silent treatment was a better strategy. Milo had a best friend, Jagger, who was a rather boisterous wheaton terrier. Whenever they got together—well, let me just say boys will be boys, much to Milan's chagrin. One day the two boys came over to visit. They tore from one end of the apartment to the other in hot pursuit of one another. Milan sniffed in disdain and watched from the sidelines, not about to cast aside her femininity and enter the fray. But then Jagger did the unspeakable. He hopped up on my bed, sniffing around as all dogs do. Milan looked at me completely mortified. I'm sure she was saying, "Do you see that? I don't even do that and I live here!"

After that she was completely disgusted and retreated from them both. Finding a comfortable spot on her favorite teddy bear she left them to wear themselves out.

Shortly thereafter Milo came sauntering over. He sniffed and she coyly turned her head away and ignored him. He got the message. Lowering himself down next to her, he put his head on his paws, looking at her very apologetically. She leaned over and sniffed his nose. Suddenly Jagger was on the outside looking in. Milan had Milo wrapped around her paw, and she hadn't said a thing. A lesson learned.

Then there was Bailey. A little unassuming-looking bichon frise, he had a major crush on Milan when she first arrived at the building. They apparently had little tete a tetes when Tim was walking her. But Milan, being the gracious little lady that she is, had enough love to share with all she met, including Marco, the havanese, who happened along when she was playing with Bailey one day. But Bailey, who was a rescue dog, was not into sharing. He couldn't bear for Milan's attention to be shifted away from him, so he went after Marco. Milan hates violence, and from that day on she would have nothing to do with Bailey. Poor Bailey was reduced to looking like a stalker. At every encounter after that they both froze, eyeing one another from a distance. Nothing could be done to repair the breach. Bailey would stare at her, but Milan refused to respond, which further incited Bailey to dislike any male who had access to her. This included Milo.

Bailey's jealousy extended beyond Milan to his owner. Poor dear, she led a pretty lonely life as Bailey's reputation for being overly protective of her preceded him. He had succeeded in shredding the pants of the condo's board president and making enemies of any other males, human or canine, that in his opinion threatened his mother. The only dog he was afraid of was Bella, a Doberman pincher, who let it be known his issues with jealousy and possessiveness were not going to be tolerated on her watch. She was not willing to share even the hallway with him. Whenever she spotted him in the vicinity she went into attack mode, completely ignoring her owner's efforts to control her. Milan's approach was to sit and wait until Bailey cleared the hall before proceeding. She was not into confrontation, and she wanted no part of those who did not pursue peace.

Milan's way with men was not limited to the canine persuasion. Her walker, Tim, adored her. Many times after walking her he would sit on the floor and play with her for a while before going on to his next appointment.

Then one day something happened between them. To this day I don't know what it was. Instead of running to the door to greet Tim when he came to walk her, she spurned him completely. To make sure there was no misunderstanding that she wanted nothing to do with him, not only did she walk away, she retreated to the leg space beneath the desk in my office. Scooting as far back as she could to make herself out of reach, she sat there avoiding his gaze and refusing to come out. We were dismayed. At first I thought she didn't want to go outside because I had traveled recently. Thinking she didn't want to leave me, I picked her up, put her leash on, and then handed it to Tim. She looked at me as if she was being led away to the guillotine.

After the third day of this I was no longer comfortable with this routine. Something was wrong and I decided to listen to my child. Tim could offer no explanation for this strange behavior and neither could Milan, but I felt I needed to followed her cues. She no longer wanted to nuzzle him. Maybe he was smoking heavily and she didn't like the smell. Who knows? But something was definitely awry.

I felt so bad when I had to tell Tim I had to let him go. He was devastated. I was apologetic, but Milan was completely detached. She'd already moved on to having a crush on another cute dog walker in the building. While I tracked him down I asked Joanne if she could squeeze Milan into her already overcrowded schedule. She acquiesced, adding her to the pack she was already walking, which included Milo.

But Joanne made it clear she couldn't add another dog to her schedule permanently because she was overbooked.

Little did I know that I was putting Joanne in the line of fire. Tim, still inconsolable from Milan's rejection, spotted Joanne walking her. This pushed him over the edge. As Joanne tells it, Tim, drunk as a skunk from the Billy Goat Tavern, called her and accused her of taking Milan away from him.

Tim then badmouthed Joanne to me, saying she was weird and kept a hundred cats at her house. I refused to hear any of it. I liked Joanne and felt she could have as many pets as she wanted because I knew her to be a meticulous caregiver. Plus Annette had told me that Joanne's place was immaculate, and in my mind insanity and uncleanliness kind of go hand in hand. She displayed neither trait as far as I could see.

In order to spare her from further harassment, I eventually hired Sayed, the cute dogwalker with the Afro that had caught Milan's eye. As I watched Milan, tail wagging happily, following him out the door for her daily midday walk I could understand why Tim would be upset and perhaps even a little jealous. He prided himself on taking good care of Milan and loving her completely. To have his love and care for her spurned caused him great pain. In his mind he was the one who loved her most. Several times after that we would run into him in the park, and he would look longingly at Milan but keep his distance. I felt bad because I didn't have the power to turn Milan's heart back to him. Only she knew how Tim had offended her. It was her decision and I couldn't discount her misgivings.

🐾 Paws to Reflect 🐾

I wonder how God feels when we spurn His affections. Have you thought about how much more gracious He is in the face of our rejection? He keeps wooing us anyway, waiting for the day when we will welcome His love and reach out to Him, ready and willing to embrace a relationship with Him.

Though I know it hurts His heart when we fail to draw close, I think perhaps He handles rejection better than we do because at the end of the day He is still the loving God who feels no need to retaliate. Our acceptance or rejection of Him does nothing to diminish, devalue, or change who He is, which is something I don't think the human mind can fathom. We feel rejection deeply and personalize it to the point of concluding that our love is somehow not valuable enough for someone else to want it. That hurts. And hurt people hurt other people.

This sense of not being affirmed or validated heightens our aggression and passion in the things of love, sometimes making us violent people, vocally or physically. We can't seem to resist the urge to strike back at people who cause us pain, especially if they've turned to someone else while rejecting us. Perhaps our own thoughts, words, and actions shock us with their ugliness in those moments. This could be the reason we equate jealousy with evil, which I don't think is always true. I think it totally depends on the motivation for jealousy and what we do with those emotions.

I once heard someone say she was really into God until one day she heard a preacher say that God was jealous. She found this rather upsetting and interpreted it as God was jealous *of* her. Of her! Can you imagine that? I thought, *How arrogant must this woman be?* To even think she had anything God could be jealous of crossed over the line to ridiculous conceit. She was neither rich nor strikingly beautiful, and even if she were, could what she had compare to who God is or what He possesses?

I totally get God's jealousy. God is jealous *over* us and not willing to share us with any other god because He knows the damage that could cause to us. He hovers protectively, passionately, and fiercely, guarding those He calls His own.

I was jealous over a man like that once. He left me for another woman, a woman I knew would never love him as deeply as I did. I lived for him. I loved him as I loved myself, and still he left me for the deceptive invitation of another. In the end I was right. She shattered and broke him completely, and he came back to me too ashamed to love me the way he should. My silence on the matter screamed at him too loudly, reminding him of the foolish choice he made. Our relationship was never the same. We faded to black, and to this day I'm still sad about what we both lost.

He failed to see the extent of my love for him until it was too late. It was so wide I couldn't get around it, so high I couldn't get over it, so deep I couldn't crawl under it, so broad I couldn't find the end of it. Oh the pain I felt when losing him.

Oh yes, I totally get the height, the breadth, the depth, the width of God's love for us. I've been there with someone who was only human, and if the truth be told I've concluded that even if God's jealousy for us was the carnal kind—the kind that is hurtful and unhealthy, the kind that most of us have toward one another for various reasons— that would still be all right. In my opinion God has the right to be jealous of our affections.

He's given us *everything,* including what is most precious to Him— His only begotten Son. Why shouldn't He expect our adoration and faithfulness in return? Is that really too much to ask when He's loved us so hard that He can't stop giving in spite of the hurt, the shame, the disappointment we have caused His heart?

What do you expect from someone when you've given him your life?

That's what I thought. *Everything* would be my response too.

14

The Unrelenting Nature of Love

One Christmas season a wave of dognappings was creating great consternation among the dog parents in my neighborhood. I was away on a speaking engagement when I got the news. Quickly I battened down the hatches, calling home to inform the dog sitter he was to stick close to home and avoid all suspicious-looking loiterers. Nine dogs were stolen by the time the news spread.

One little boy was completely traumatized by his experience. He was walking his dog when a man got out of a van idling on the corner. The man lowered himself to pet the dog. The boy, sensing something was wrong, pulled his dog away but the man grabbed it, unhooked the dog's leash, scooped him up, jumped into the waiting van, and sped away. I couldn't believe it! I had images of myself on the hood of a car holding on for dear life should that happen with Milan. Imagine the distress this poor little boy experienced!

Upon my return home I saw signs posted everywhere offering a reward for the safe return of Lola, a cute Norwich terrier, "last seen wearing a green pea coat." Lola had been snatched from the backseat of her parent's car. The woman was inconsolable. For a while she was not only distraught at the loss of her dog but riddled with guilt believing she had failed to lock the car. Upon further investigation she discovered the lock had been broken. Her search for her beloved little girl was unrelenting. she reported her misfortune to the police, only to be told rather casually that there had been several dognappings in the area. It seemed that little dogs were being taken to either be given as gifts for

Christmas or an even more sinister and ugly reason—to be used as bait at dogfights. This latter information pushed me over the edge. I was on my way to Africa, and there was no way I was leaving Milan in the neighborhood to be easy prey without me to protect her. I shuttled her off to the home of one of her teachers, LaRue, on the South Side where I knew she would be safe until my return. Of course I still made a hundred calls over the holidays to check on her welfare.

Meanwhile the owners of the missing dogs weren't taking this travesty lying down. They were staging major campaigns in search of their lost loved ones. The little boy's story received the attention of the news media, and after reading a newspaper article someone called to report he believed he'd bought the dog in question from its kidnapper. He then orchestrated its safe return. The little boy's parents not only reimbursed the guy the $300 he had paid for the dog, but rewarded him with an additional $500. I could relate to that. I would easily have paid for Milan all over again if someone held her for ransom. And she wasn't cheap.

Lola's story wasn't so easily resolved. For months her owner searched high and low, wandering through the neighborhood, even venturing into a nearby housing project where no one dared go alone. Her flyers were everywhere, offering a generous reward.

After eight months of working intensely with the authorities, a neighbor of the dognapper called to report Lola's whereabouts! Ironically the thief was already in jail for slashing and attacking passersby in the Edgewater area of town. He had taken Lola as a gift for his daughter. Unbelievable! Poor Lola didn't recognize her mother by the time she was saved and returned, but the woman was happy to have Lola back nonetheless. They are doing just fine now. Their experience made us all more aware and wiser, causing us to be on guard lest we suffer the same loss without such a happy ending.

Paws to Reflect

There's no describing the pain of loss even though it can vary in degree, depending on the value of what's been lost. I've been haunted by something I misplaced simply because I didn't want to accept that I'd been careless enough to put it in the wrong place. I found it a year later, and my elation was overwhelming. My faith in the power of persistence was restored. But some lost things are irretrievable, and you wonder at your capacity to bounce back. When it's a loved one that's suddenly gone it's unspeakable torment.

I lost someone like that once. The man I loved. Scotty. He was beautiful. When he smiled the sun rose in the room. His laughter was deep and contagious. When he held me, I felt secure. His passion was genuine and palpable, and I knew he loved me. But one day he was gone. Lost. A bullet came between us. Ripping his internal organs and shattering my heart.

I remember when I got the call that he was gone. I had been out celebrating getting hired for my first real job at a prestigious ad agency. Fresh out of school I'd been instrumental in them winning a coveted account. My prize was a promotion from freelance work to a permanent position. I was over the moon. But shortly after arriving home my pleasure was exchanged for the most immense pain I've ever experienced.

"Where have you been?" his aunt asked when I returned her phone call. Then she told me, "He's gone, Michelle. We've been trying to call you all afternoon." I don't think I heard anything else she said after that. It was white noise as I felt myself descending, falling into a black hole that had no bottom, no cushion. I hit bottom and lay there in the silence trying to feel something—my feet, my heart, anything—but I felt nothing but pain. Nothing but loss. It was so thick it smelled. A part of me had been severed suddenly and violently, leaving a gaping, bleeding hole I couldn't quite locate to cleanse.

Then I remember trying to stand from the seat where I'd been sitting but my equilibrium was askew, my balance off. Yes, of course, because a part of me was missing. I had been cut in two. I couldn't breathe. Couldn't see where I was or beyond the moment. I couldn't see my future without Scotty. I wanted to die. I vaguely remember hanging up and calling Brenda from next door to come and sit with me, although at the time we weren't even close friends. She called Michelle for reinforcement. Together we sat in silence. They knew there was nothing anyone could say.

I couldn't cry. I was crushed beneath my agony, concentrating on taking one breath after another, searching for the end of my nightmare. I didn't know God at that time, so I didn't think to have a conversation with Him about this. I had to solve this by myself. But I was young and too new to life to consider death with all its implications.

Scotty had hovered between life and death for a month, and now the story had ended in a way I wasn't ready for. I had played out all the possible scenarios in my head, hoping against hope against this particular conclusion. I had lost him. But where was he? Would I ever see him again? I couldn't bear the thought of never touching him again, never feeling strong because of his wanting me again. The more I thought of these things the more my pain grew.

I moved through the pain day after day floating on a cloud of Valium, trying to anticipate when I would crash so I could prop myself up with a drink in enough time to cushion the fall. I questioned my sanity, fearing I was losing more than just Scotty's love.

And then I had a dream. In the dream I was walking down a lonely street that ran in front of a church. I could hear a choir singing the closer I got to the church. Their praise surrounded me, easing my pain, but I didn't go in. I sat on a bench outside, letting the music wash over me until my pain was completely gone. Then I got up and walked away. As the voices of the choir faded, my pain returned. I wondered after I woke up if this was some divine message that I needed to go back to church, but my pain engulfed me, drowning out all possibility of comfort. Eventually I did go back to church and the vision proved true. I found myself and all my missing parts in the arms of Jesus.

Jesus washed me and held me and absorbed all my pain, anger, and fear. He replaced death with new life, infusing it into my heart, soul, and spirit. It wouldn't be until much later that I would truly consider

His joy at reclaiming me. I was lost in my own ideas, values, and bad choices before I turned to Him.

He left heaven to come looking for me. I was just like that woman at the well in Samaria, jaded and settling for far less than she should, not able to recognize a blessing when it stood in front of her. I was lost while I wandered, looking for love in all the wrong places and finally finding it, only to have it unceremoniously ripped from the center of my life. I was a lost, empty mess. And still Jesus came, calling after me, following the path of my tears, stepping over my foolishness, wading through all the filthy things I'd ever said and done, marking a path through my despair. He stopped at the cross long enough to embrace my pain and pay the final ransom—His life—for me that cost way more than I was really worth.

But even that didn't stop Him. He just kept coming. Past death, past hell, past eternity. He was relentless in His search for me, which was really my search for Him, though I didn't know it until I landed at His feet, clutching the foot of the cross, hopeless, empty, broken, and spent.

No one has to tell me about being lost and losing things. I've experienced both. Losing, finding, being lost, being found. Still I can't really say why the relief is so great when we reach the end of our trouble. Perhaps the reward of gaining what we've lost is only as great as the intensity of our search? I have no real answers. All I can tell you is that restoration is powerful and beautiful and changes everything.

When I returned from Africa the joy I felt when I scooped Milan into my arms can't be expressed. She was still there waiting for me. I couldn't imagine coming home to find her gone. Taken away by someone who would never understand what she meant to me. Never again would I take her presence in my life for granted.

I realized the full import that tomorrow is not promised. But also that neither death nor life, angels nor demons, the present nor the future, or powers of any height or depth, or anything in creation can separate me from the love of God that is in Christ Jesus, who keeps helping us all find our way back home.

SoundBite
He Is Faithful

"Dog is God spelled backward." That saying has always disturbed me. To compare God to a dog seems sacrilegious...until I look beneath the surface. This was brought home to me by a story my assistant, Rachel, told me. When she was in school she knew some boys who owned a blind dog named Sadie. They delighted in calling her and then moving out of the way so that when she came she would bump into walls and furniture.

They thought it was funny that no matter how many times they called her, no matter where they led her, she would come every time. She was that faithful and trusting. Perhaps she, like many who have given their hearts to the wrong people, hoped the next time would be different. Or her unconditional love made her respond to their call no matter how cruel their intentions. That's what true love does. I'm not saying true love is blind. Far from it. God *is* love and the *source* of love, and He is not blind at all. He sees us very clearly.

God has simply chosen not to linger over the problem (our disobedience) but focus on the solution (our salvation). God knows that divine love is the solution. Love champions the beloved to become better than they are, loving in spite of the flaws because it focuses on the perfect work we will become when won over and shaped by love. And so Love (God) keeps believing, hoping, and remaining faithful even when we are faithless by wandering and making everything else our first love. The source of love (God again!) is faithful, patiently waiting for us to exhaust ourselves and find our way back to Him.

I love the fact that Milan and Matisse will welcome anyone, play with anyone...but if they think I'm about to leave, their eyes fix on me. No matter what anybody says, no matter where they invite them to go, they won't budge. If it looks like I'm leaving them, they forsake whatever is being offered and follow me. I am their universe, their sun, their moon, their all. Life for them begins and ends with me. They can't bear to be separated from me. At the end of the day no diversion or distraction takes the place of my loving arms. How is that for faithfulness? And their faithfulness makes me want to be a better person, to care for them, protect them, love them more. It's my way of reciprocating the love and steadfast devotion they give to me.

That's what faithfulness does. It puts everything in perspective and uncovers our inconsistencies and our need to draw nearer to God, who is most faithful of all, the true beginning and end, the moon, the stars and the Son. God. He owes me nothing more because He's given me everything by giving me Himself.

Now it's my turn. I fully realize that my faithfulness will grow in degrees, unfortunately more through the things I suffer than by my voluntary volition to stay and not to stray. But hopefully the learning curve will flatten as I go along. The comforting truth is whether I do or don't, even so He is faithful.

15

The Danger of Judging Others

I hated my assistant's dog. Yes, I said it. I *hated* him. He was bad. Like those unruly children you see at the mall screaming, yelling, and flinging themselves on the ground, embarrassing their parents, who never seem to have the courage to correct them in public lest they get arrested. You don't know who you want to throttle most—the parents or the child.

Crystal, my assistant at the time, wanted to get a dog and wondered if she could bring it to work with her. In the moment, it seemed like a good idea. After all, it would be great company for Milan, who had been spending entire days napping and gaining weight from lack of activity.

Once I gave her the green light my assistant ignored all of my advice on how to select the right puppy and went to work looking for a dog on the internet. She found a breeder for silver-haired terriers out of state and oohed and aahed over all the cute photos.

"Never buy a dog sight unseen," I cautioned her. "You need to see the dogs in person, in their environment before you pick one. That way you can observe their temperaments." This went over her head. She was totally caught up in anticipation, and before I could give further input she had arranged to have the dog flown in.

"Big mistake," I muttered under my breath. This comment too evaporated into thin air, along with my question about the breeder who was releasing a dog to fly at eight weeks old. Any breeder worth their reputation didn't release puppies before 12 weeks of age.

Morocco started off cute enough, just like any new relationship. A small round bundle of fur. He was such a cute puppy. I was the one who named him. He arrived in a tiny crate filled with sawdust. He was so adorable and fluffy I almost wanted another puppy myself. Milan was filled with wonder, gazing at him as he settled into the office peacefully sleeping in his crate, being released only to go outside for a piddle. Milan would press her nose against the door of his crate to visit, and they commiserated quietly throughout the day. So far so good.

But then Morocco grew. And grew. Crystal had proudly announced that he was a toy terrier and would only reach the weight of four pounds at the most. I voiced my doubts. How could she really know? She hadn't seen the parents or gone to see the breeders in person. A breeder can tell you anything over the phone. Another red flag was that Morocco's price was way too low if all the breeder claimed about his pedigree was true.

As it turned out, Morocco was indeed not a toy terrier. He was a toy terrorist. Strong-willed and defiant, he delighted in piddling on my leather rug any time he got the opportunity. That activity quickly got him banished to his cage during working hours—much to Milan's displeasure.

But whenever he was released to play with her he lunged at her face, snipping and snapping until we had to separate them. That sort of behavior earned him a ticket to boot camp with LaRue, Milan's old trainer and babysitter. The training worked—but only at LaRue's. Once he was reunited with his mother he resorted to his rebellious ways.

I tried to like him. I really did. Once I invited him over to play with Milan at my house. He started off playing nicely but then again snipped and snapped at Milan's face, so I put him in Milan's piddle station for a time out.

A lot of good that did. Morocco scaled the top of the pen and landed, defiantly planting his feet in the middle of the pathway between my living room and dining room. He promptly squatted and deliberated peed in the middle of the floor while looking at me angrily!

Milan cocked her head at me in horror, waiting to see my reaction.

As I stood looking at him a vision passed before my eyes of me flipping him over the banister of my balcony into the river and telling his mother I didn't know what had happened. Since everyone knew his amazing ability to leap over things, I could easily have gotten away with saying, "I just turned around and he was gone!" Instead I drew a deep breath and banished him from my home.

"Can't you do anything with him?" I asked LaRue, who just hunched his shoulders and said, "I don't have any problems with Morocco. He knows he can't get away with that stuff with me. It's all his mother's fault."

At this point I think Crystal was in complete denial, as many mothers are about their children. "I don't know what happens," she said with wide-eyed innocence. "He's so good at home. It's not until he comes to the office that he acts up."

"Good according to whose standards?" I asked. "Crystal, you're not disciplining him properly. Milan would never do the things *he* does."

Okay, so I was self-righteous and judgmental because I had the perfect child. I didn't understand why she couldn't get her dog to behave like Milan. The more I thought about it, the more my attitude changed from a loving aunt to disapproving observer. Morocco clearly got the message. I could tell by the way he looked at me that there was no love lost between us. This also put a strain on my relationship with Crystal. When she later left (for totally unrelated reasons), it was a relief. Peace had been restored...or so I thought.

Having Morocco in the office had clarified one thing in my mind—Milan needed company. Yes Milo was still a steady play date, but he was moving to New York. So on that note I called Milan's breeder, Daryl, to find out when she would have another litter ready for adoption. She told me she had just gotten a new litter, which included a little boy who was so gorgeous she was thinking about keeping him for show, but I could come and look at him if I wanted. Off to the breeder's I went again.

Daryl was right. The puppy was absolutely beautiful. White and deep auburn with black tips, he was still too small for me to touch him, but he quickly moved me from my resolve to acquire another girl I planned to name Simone after singer Nina Simone.

Annette had been campaigning for me to get a boy from the beginning. "The girls are too independent, too much like cats," she said. "Boys are lovers. They just love you more. You'll be happier."

I hadn't been convinced until now. This guy was just so cu-ute and cuddly! (Yes, I've also said that about countless men who turned out not to be so cute and cuddly.)

"I'll take him!" I did have a moment of trepidation when I called to check on him a month later and she replied, "Oh, he's here attacking his mother." When I asked what that meant she gave me a very

vague statement about him being "feisty." I wasn't sure what that meant, but since his mother was Milan's grandmother I dismissed my fears with the rationale that he came from good stock and, after all, he was a boy, so he was supposed to be a little more active. Yeah, yeah, that's the ticket. It sounded good at the time.

And so on April first (there was something prophetic about picking him up on April Fools' day) Matisse came home and another adventure began. But this one had a bumpy start. It was as if Matisse was Morocco's revenge. My new boy was nothing like Milan. For one thing, he was a barker who didn't like being contained. The moment I put him into his crate at the foot of my bed that first night he started his loud, sharp protests. Milan sidled up to the crate, nudging him in her motherly way to encourage him to calm down, but he would not be silenced.

She then lay down next to the crate, as if to assure him that even though he wasn't free to roam, she was nearby. Still he wouldn't be comforted. Milan rolled over on her side, demonstrating that he should follow suit. But he wasn't interested in calming down at all. His barking echoed off the ceiling and filled the room. It reminded me of a jackhammer from a construction site.

After a while Milan gave up and sauntered away, following me to my bed for comfort. From her perch on the bed she looked down at him as if to say, "If you would be quiet you could be up here too." I think it made him even madder.

When I told Annette about it later, she got a big kick out of it. She called him a little…well, I'll give you a hint: One of my friends said I got a shih tzu so I could curse without having to ask for forgiveness.

Milan had taken three weeks to earn her freedom and know where to piddle. But Matisse wasn't about to be taught. He had no regard for being corrected. He was bent on doing *what* he wanted, *where* he wanted. So I shuttled him off to Good Dog for training. A full course for 30 days of dropping him off in the morning and picking him up at the end of the day. The good news was they told me he was smart and good. The bad news was that he was only that way at school. At home he did everything I disdained in the behavior of other people's dogs.

Matisse had a lot of "accidents," though I felt they were on purpose. And he chewed on things! Milan had never done that. I accused her of deluding me into thinking all dogs were as sweet as she was. Okay, I admit it. I had prided myself on raising the perfect dog, and now I was being tested, coming face-to-face with my limitations. I was not a happy camper.

Matisse was not the cool, calm, confident cucumber Milan was. Perhaps he had abandonment issues from the death of his sibling. I don't know that, but I do know he was orally fixated (he had to taste and lick everything) and extremely prideful. He knew he was beautiful and everyone around him reinforced this by constantly telling him so. It took us forever to get down the street because he literally stopped traffic. Head held high, hair flowing in the breeze, he preened for his observers. He was also opinionated and barked back when corrected.

Matisse was his own dog. Life was all about him. He couldn't bear to share the attention, and that resulted in him terrorizing poor Milan. Milan looked at me rather accusingly, as if to say, "Whose brilliant idea was it to bring this crazy dog into the house?" On that note she completely dissed him. Milan and her boyfriend, Milo, soon decided Matisse was beneath them. They formed their own two-dog clique, which totally frustrated Matisse, causing him to try to muscle into their space even harder.

Our world was turned upside down by our tiny new little family member. I fluctuated between how cute he was and how bad he was, finally falling into the same syndrome as all the other mothers who try to justify their bad child's behavior. My weak rationalization was "after all he's just a puppy." The truth was that I was finally experiencing everything I had judged others about. My words, "Why can't she get her dog under control?" came back to haunt me. Now I was the guilty party.

One day I sat looking at Matisse and thought, *Perhaps I've bitten off more than I can chew. Maybe I should take him back.* Then I started calculating how much I had spent on him. Vet visits. Shots. Training. Fancy leash and collar. All the paraphernalia that goes with spoiling a dog. I might have been able to get back what I'd purchased him for, but that wouldn't make up for half of what I'd spent afterward. I just couldn't do it. I couldn't give up on him or give him back. I had invested too much in him. And that's when I heard it loud and clear as a bell. The voice of God saying, "Michelle, that's exactly how I feel about you. I can't give up on you either. I've invested way too much in you. Do not judge, or you too will be judged."

Wow! You could have knocked me over with a feather. That's when I got it. God would withhold judgment of me, giving me more chances than I deserved to become what He wants me to be because of what He's invested in me. Because He gave His most precious possession to purchase me, He couldn't make what Jesus had done for me on the cross meaningless and valueless by turning His back when I made a mistake. Just because I was flawed and imperfect wasn't enough of an incentive for Him to decree me hopeless enough to give up on.

After all I am only human.

Paws to Reflect

If God withholds judgment, giving everyone plenty of opportunities to get their acts together, who am I to judge others? Yes, I have the right to judge in the sense of discerning if someone's actions are right or wrong, but I don't have the right to decide what people's punishments will be or to give up on them. My God-given duty is to give others the same chances God gives me to redeem myself or at least cling to the redemption Christ offers.

Life is one long journey of becoming, where we evolve through the lessons we learn (or don't learn). At any given time we're all sitting in different classrooms in the school of life. I can't force you to learn my lesson if that's not the course God has for you. And I certainly can't give you failing marks if you never took the class I just finished. That doesn't mean you won't eventually get there, but you're just not there right now—and that's all right.

Getting to this place was the hard part. I've been guilty of judging others and being quite vocal about what I felt they deserved for their actions. Ah, but all things come to light eventually, and God has an interesting sense of humor when it comes to dealing with us when we begin to think too much of ourselves.

Sometimes our critical judgments of others come from a place of deep-green envy. Is it possible that the Pharisees were just a little jealous of the sin they accused others of? You better believe it. They had to toe the line as part of their job description, though it was against their nature to be that upright.

They struggled beneath the rules they inflicted on others, and it made them harsh and evil. If they weren't having fun no one else would either! I've been there. Like the fox walking away from the grapes he couldn't reach in Aesop's fable, I've decreed the unreachable as "sour" in an effort to comfort myself over what I felt I was missing. I've looked through the window of longing, wondering how others seemed to get away with things God wouldn't let me do. And even though I knew it was sin and was aware of the eventual fallout, I envied their freedom while fearing the consequences enough not to follow their example. I've decreed those people were going to hell in a handbasket because *I* was a good little Christian do-bee and *they* were not.

There it is. Judgment that stinks to high heaven all dressed up under the guise of righteousness. Like the publican praying in public, "Oh God, I thank you that I am not like *those* people" (even though some small part of me wishes I were, if the truth be told).

Someone once said God doesn't like ugly. Well, He doesn't care for pretty that much either, especially if you're "smelling yourself," as the old folks used to say. (That means thinking you're a bit more special than everyone else.)

I've heard God say to me, "You are right but you are wrong," meaning I've stepped into territory that I'm not allowed to enter lest I find myself in deeper trouble than I ever imagined. I've learned that "I would never do that" are dangerous words because no one knows what they would do in a given situation until he or she is there. And if you want to find out what you're truly made of, just judge someone else. God will make sure you end up in the same situation to make you eat your words and help you become a little more humble.

The quicker we learn this lesson the better off we'll be: No two people (or dogs) are alike. It's not fair to expect more from a person than he or she is capable of producing. That's perhaps why God is infinitely more patient with us than we are with one another.

Realizing this convicted me and made me more accepting of Matisse. I got rid of the harsh lens of my perfect expectations that were robbing me of the ability to see the good qualities he did have. My judgment was keeping us from bonding. Matisse sensed my disdain and acted up even more. When I finally relaxed, I was amazed as he began to respond to my acceptance by seeking to please me instead of defying me. I got past the shock of how different he was from Milan and began to delight in his uniqueness.

Milan was a phlegmatic, easygoing temperament. Matisse was classically sanguine, emotional, and outgoing. Milan was a meanderer; Matisse was a sprinter. They were like day and night. Low energy, high energy. Teachable and obedient, obstinate and wayward. Cautious and tentative, adventurous in the moment, easily distracted and throwing caution to the wind. Milan was the consummate little lady, prim and proper. Matisse was like a little rock star. Even his hair rebelled. I started calling him Keith Richards because of how his hair stood on end. The diva and the rebel. It was like living with a split personality. *My* split personality, if you must know.

I was talking on the phone one day and one of my friends asked, "Is Milan there? I've heard you call Matisse at least ten times since we started talking, and you haven't said Milan once!" I had to admit that Matisse got more attention because he demanded it. He was my special-needs child. He needed more of everything. More food. More exercise. More attention. More love...and he didn't stop until he got it. I had to respect him for that. He wormed his way into the hearts of everyone, and the deeper my love grew for him the more amenable I became to his personality. Love does cover a multitude of sins!

And this is where I found the secret to freeing myself from being judgmental. I realized the more I loved Matisse the less I wanted to punish him and the more I wanted to take the time to help him be the best he could be—to lovingly train and instruct him. When he messed up I was quick to forgive him and get him back on track.

The struggle with judgment comes from lack of love. You see, I hadn't loved Morocco. He wasn't mine and ultimately wasn't my concern. I had responded to him with impatience and the urge to kill. The situation was really more about me than it was about him.

I love Matisse, and he is mine. Just like a mother who can love a wayward child in spite of all his or her wicked ways and the crimes committed, love blots out judgment. Love kills the temptation to jump to the conclusion that the loved one is unredeemable. It hopes against hope for the greater good of the person loved. Love doesn't render a sentence because it keeps expecting, keeps hoping, keeps believing for the one loved to finally "get it" and live up to his or her greatest potential. To overcome every flaw and be gloriously transformed into something truly beautiful.

That's deep. God loves me, God owns me, and He has the same hope for me that I harbor for Matisse and several others in my life: a butterfly moment where we all will shed the cumbersome chrysalis of ourselves and fly above the wreckage, free from failure and the judgment it invites.

16

The Contagious Nature of Sin

I was on the phone with my mother when the call came from Marilyn at Good Dog. "Did you hear Milan coughing this morning before you brought her to school?"

No, I had not.

Marilyn suspected she had kennel cough. It had been going around. She recommended that I pick up Milan, take her to the doctor, and not bring her back to school until the contagious period had passed lest she pass it on to the other dogs.

My mother couldn't believe the fuss. "You sound as if you're dealing with a child! Can dogs be contagious?" I assured her they were indeed little children, and yes, they could also pass colds as well as bad habits among one another…just like humans.

The next several days were spent trying to keep Milan, Matisse, and Milo, who was living with us for several weeks before moving to New York, apart long enough for the contagious period to pass. But as you can guess, the cough traveled, and everyone had a bout of it before it all ended.

The other interesting thing that happened during this time is that I'd been counting on Milan to train Matisse in her good habits. But instead she began to pick up Matisse's bad habits. I caught her in mid pee in the middle of my white living room rug. When I fussed at her about it she looked at me as if to say, "Well, Matisse does it all the time, why can't I?"

"Because you know better!" was my answer before putting her in her pen for a time out. She sat there letting me know her punishment was completely unfair. I took the time to tell her she was the older sibling and should be teaching Matisse how to behave and not following his bad example. She seemed to understand and after that incident she never did it again. Interestingly, Matisse's accidents soon subsided too.

Someone once asked me how I knew who had done what if I had two dogs. I laughed as I shared how the guilty party always gave it away. As I stood in the middle of the house with my hand on my hip indignantly pointing to the crime, one of them was sure to bow their head and slink away, silently exposing his or her guilt. The remorse in the dog's eyes was undeniable, but just like children, I suppose, in the moment it seemed like a good idea to do whatever they wanted, to piddle where they pleased, or completely annihilate a piece of paper.

I found it interesting that the one bad habit that never transferred to Milan from Matisse was chewing up things. Milan never chewed my shoes or anything that was not given to her. Matisse, however, had to taste and chew *everything*. The legs of barstools, shoes, the corner of a desk, my Bic shaver (I was horrified at the potential for injury but saw no signs of blood). You name it, Matisse chewed it. Anything I treasured had to be put out of reach. It was open season on any unsuspecting article that looked tasty. This didn't faze Milan at all. She preferred real food.

After several visits at Milo's house I noticed Milan had taken to watching me accusingly while I ate. She had never done this in the past. Yes, it was official. She was begging. Though I told her this was totally unattractive, she persisted. My answer was to ignore her until she got the message that no people food would be passing her lips. The vet said it wasn't good for her, and I had no intention of loving her to death.

Then I noticed Annette shared her food with Milo. *Aha!* So this is where Milan picked this idea up. Milo begged so Milan followed suit.

Annette wasn't interested in my dissertation about people food not being good for dogs. She just sighed and said it was too late. She'd already spoiled Milo, and there could be or would be no turning back. Besides, he just loved mushrooms. Asking her not to give Milo people food in front of Milan fell on deaf ears too. It was *my* problem. If I wanted to deprive Milan that was too bad, but she would not deny Milo. And so Milan was destined to wonder about people food unless she was sick and bland chicken and rice was prescribed to settle her stomach.

If it's true that bad company corrupts good morals I suppose the reverse should also be true—that good behavior engenders good behavior in others...but I've found that often isn't the case.

Paws to Reflect

What one person does eventually affects countless others. That's life. One person decides to bomb a plane with his shoe, so now we all have to take our shoes off when going through security at the airport. It's changed the way the world travels forever. This is the truth across the board in every area of life, from fashion trends to the way we do business, from the way we play to how we live out our faith.

I knew of a church once where it was uncovered that one of the men in leadership was having an affair. The next thing I heard was that many marriages in the church were disintegrating, as if his failure gave everyone else permission to also fall. When he lowered the bar a lot of people ducked under it. It was like a cancer spreading throughout the entire body. Sometimes I think this is true of the church at large too. I see the standards of believers vacillating as they try to assimilate into the world more and more. In the interest of getting along with everybody, standards get lowered and compromises are made.

Paul the apostle talked about a little leaven leavening the whole lump. He warned about the damage of cashing in our faith for immediate treats that could spoil things for everyone. Like the ripples a stone incites when it hits the water, one person's fall eventually gets many wet in some way. Sin may taste good and be pleasurable for a season, but it makes people sick in the end. The church looks bad as a whole when everyone starts slipping and sliding, living below the standards God has set and those the world expects from us.

Respect is lost over the disgrace of yet another fallen believer or Christian leader, and someone rejects the truth because the excuse is given that no one is really living it. Someone misses out on eternity because of a bad example.

I don't know about you, but I don't want to have to answer for that. The end result of compromise or sin is never worth the few moments of gratification. And it usually takes much longer to repair the damage.

I find it even stranger that almost everyone believes they will escape the consequences of their actions. But that is the pull of sin. Sin is desirable. Even the Bible says sin is pleasurable for a season. Sin whispers, "Let's think about the consequences *after* the enjoyment is over." The bottom line is we all choose our pain according to what we like. This extends beyond the church to groups, affiliations, and all the way to individuals.

As I tried to decipher what caused Milan to be amenable to some of Matisse's antics and totally averse to others, I realized she was only tempted in the areas where she was already susceptible—mainly anything having to do with food. Milan loved to eat; therefore, she was always grappling with her weight, just like her mother. Ahem, that would be me. I noticed when I gained weight, so did she. When I lost weight...you guessed it.

Whenever she saw me eating she took it as a cue that she should be eating too. When it came to food or her personal comfort, she could be swayed to follow anyone's lead who seemed to have a way of getting what she wanted. Therefore, begging and relieving herself in inappropriate places were behaviors I focused on correcting.

Temptation is an interesting animal. It's powerless if you're not interested. However, if you have the slightest bent toward its invitation, you've lost the fight—unless you're wise enough to realize what's going on and where you're being led. I avoid shoe sales because I know that even if I don't need another pair of shoes, I will fall prey to the markdown because my love for shoes will overrule what I know to be the right thing to do—not buy them.

I can only be tempted where desire, interest, or curiosity for what is being offered is already present. So it stands to reason that if I'm satisfied with my meal, another piece of dessert can't tempt me, no matter how much I love what is being served. Unlike Matisse, Milan didn't feel the need to be admired by other people because she already felt loved and nurtured. But Matisse is always reaching for more attention. No matter how much I give him, he feels the need to reach out for additional sustenance. He is more susceptible to being led astray by an attentive stranger. Understanding how temptation works can really help if we're willing to be honest about our weaknesses and needs.

In the Bible, when Satan tempted Jesus, he tried to get Him in the same areas he tantalizes us—the lust of the eyes, the lust of the flesh, and the pride of life. First he offered Jesus food because He had just finished fasting for 40 days. But Jesus wasn't moved because He was full from another source. He understood that if His spiritual hunger was satisfied, His physical hunger would acquiesce to the greater power.

I've learned that in the midst of my rummaging through my refrigerator for another snack, many times I'm spiritually hungry. When I don't follow the cues of my spirit to seek more of God, the void inside grows until it becomes a rumbling voice that misguides me to shop, eat, partake of things that only increase my hunger. And by the time I'm finished partaking, I'm staring at the consequences of seemingly harmless distractions. I, like Milan, can be totally driven by my appetite, not stopping until I've satisfied the desire of my flesh, no matter how much my spirit warns against it.

Back in the desert, Satan then appealed to Jesus' ego, taunting Him to prove who He was. But Jesus knew who He was and didn't feel the need for validation from anyone else. This sense of knowing who He was kept Him silent in front of those who would falsely accuse Him later and embolden Him to say, "No one takes [my life] from me, but I lay it down of my own accord."

Wow! I soooo want to be there, but I'm just not that humble. I want to be, but I'm not. Don't get me wrong, most people say I'm down-to-earth and humble, but at the end of the day if I'm pushed, I insist on my rights. I demand to be heard when I feel my rights are being violated. Sometimes I'm able to hold my peace and let God fight my battles, but I still haven't totally mastered the art of letting go and being silent. I'm naturally a fighter.

I once heard someone say that he was humble, and it was all I could do to just press my lips together and shake my head. I wanted to scream, "Honey, you are *not* humble! A humble person never thinks he is humble enough to utter it." But I was on good behavior that day, thank the Lord.

Pride is ugly and defiling. It makes us look ridiculous and say stupid things in attempts to prove our worth. It screams, "Look at me! I'm all that and a bag of chips, don't you agree?" What's really being said is, "I need you to think highly of me so I can feel good about myself. Please tell me I'm great so I can begin to believe it." Jesus didn't need that, and He wasn't tempted in the least to make Himself look like a hotshot in Satan's eyes. Nope, He didn't need the devil's approval. He had His Father's approval, and His Father is God.

And last but not least, Satan tempted Jesus through the lust of the eyes. Have your eyes ever been larger than your stomach? I have several friends who are QVC Network junkies. They're always complaining about how they have to stop watching because they always see something to buy! Well du-uh. There is no way to mindlessly watch people wagging fabulous things you love under your nose and not want to reach out and touch...and own.

Satan was offering Jesus something He knew He already owned— the world. If Jesus had to humble Himself to get it back—to get us back—He was cool with that because He was focused on the end of the matter. The part where He would be back on the throne welcoming us home. You see, when I think about the size ten dress I want to get into, I can turn down a piece of cake. Because of what I'm focused on I can squeeze past a momentary fix.

Jesus had a clear idea of where He was going, the result He wanted, what He already had, and who He was in the scheme of the struggle. When I think of life this way, I finally get to the core of how to win my fight over temptation.

God cannot be tempted because everything He wants or needs is already contained within Himself. That's it! I get in trouble when I think I need more than what I already possess. When I doubt my value and significance, my beauty, talent, abilities, and even desirability, I reach for fulfillment in sometimes awkward ways that sabotage the very thing I'm trying to lay hold of. Am I not a basket case? Okay, don't answer that.

All this comes to light when I watch Milan looking for another bite when she's just been fed. She doesn't believe I'll ever feed her again.

And then when I see Matisse struggling for more reassurance that he is loved I shake my head and realize my dogs and I suffer from the same insecurities.

From the outside looking in, I know I love them more than they can contain and that I will faithfully feed them and care for them. All they have to do is obey me. Even if they don't, I'll still take care of them. Now if I could have that same attitude about God's love toward me…knowing and believing that because He is my owner, I too have everything I need—nothing more, nothing less. If I could grasp hold of the truth that He will *always* supply my daily bread, faithfully and patiently in spite of my lack of assurance or obedience from time to time, it would relieve my anxiety.

I'm struck with a profound thought: Only God fulfills. Nothing and no one else does. Simple but amazing!

I am His and He is mine; therefore, I have everything.

SoundBite
A Matter of Taste

If you don't plan on giving your dog people food for the rest of its life, it's best not to start at all. Once when Milan and Matisse were experiencing a bout of irritable bowel and diarrhea, Dr. Schule instructed me to give them boiled chicken breast and rice to settle their stomachs. When their condition persisted, he put them on a bland, canned food formula. They absolutely loved it! It was something new to tickle their palate.

After their condition improved they were loathe to return to their regular dry formula food. They sniffed at it disdainfully while eyeing me as if to say, "Hey, where's the good stuff?" It took trickery to get them to go back to their normal diet. I mixed the old with the new until they were weaned off the wet food and back to the crunchy stuff. Matisse held out the longest, finally giving in because of the fear of starvation.

Isn't it interesting how our appetites adapt? Try going back to discount shoes after slipping into a pair of Manola Blahniks, or any designer shoes for that matter. Now that you've had a taste of the finer things, suddenly the bar is raised and you are loathe to settle for less than the best again.

Now let's flip the script. Try fasting. Strip your diet of sugar, dairy, and salt for a week. One taste of sugar is all it takes to send you reeling back into bad habits. Why is it so much easier to embrace bad habits than establish and keep good ones? It comes down to what we crave. Some of us find out the hard way that what's good *to* us is not necessarily good *for* us.

If you have champagne taste on a beer budget, though designer shoes may feel wonderful, they wreak havoc on your wallet. Sugar is sweet, but too much of even a good thing can cause you major health problems. Though I know Milan and Matisse would much rather have people food, I deny them that luxury. Call me mean, but I call it love. I know it's not good for them long term. So even though they look pitiful and try to make me feel guilty, I don't bow to pooch manipulation.

Like a parent who knows what's best for their child and stands firm not giving into the tears and tantrums, God chooses carefully what He allows us to feast on...if we submit to His diet plan. Knowing that we have free will and the right to choose what we feed our spirits, minds, and bodies, He urges us not to spend money on what isn't good for us. Instead He encourages us to eat His Word so that our souls can delight themselves in abundant, nutritious fare. He knows that His Words feed us life, health, and strength. They give us joy that refuels our energy, wisdom to make right choices, and the power to endure all things.

This may sound a lot like eating broccoli while you're eyeing something a little more spicy. Maybe you're in a relationship that's sure to do more damage than good. Or a bad habit keeps you in a cycle of defeat. It's hard to let go of what feeds your flesh even though it may starve your soul.

Recently I went to Jenny Craig. One of the secrets they teach is to fill up on the good things—vegetables and fruits—to curb hunger and keep from eating the things that create fat. Hmm, perhaps that's why the psalmist said, "Oh taste and see that God is good." What God serves is filling. No empty calories, no health problems—just life and more life.

We get to choose every day. Life or death, blessing or curses. I've come to the conclusion that making the right choices that satisfy and feed us always comes down to a matter of taste.

17

The Key to Going Places in Life

One of my occupational and relational hazards is that I travel a lot. So much so that several of my male friends have said they wouldn't date me because I'm never home.

When Milan came into my life I included her in my travel plans if I was going to be gone more than two days and not traveling overseas. In those cases I left her in the care of her teachers at the boarding school. The first time I left her for a three-week trip I wept. She told me with a look, "You're not really leaving me…are you?" I'm sure she did!

I felt so guilty I could hardly stand it. But the alternative wasn't practical. Taking her to Ghana would require six months in quarantine, which was much longer than I planned on staying. School was the best alternative. I knew she would be well cared for, her good training maintained, and a set routine established. So off to Good Dog she went.

Upon my return Milan was ecstatic to see me. She slept on my bed for an entire week! She followed me closely everywhere. I suspect she wasn't willing to let me out of her sight lest I decide to take off again.

From that day on, anytime I rolled out my large suitcase she would throw up and get diarrhea. Now that's some kind of love. I haven't met a man yet who will throw up if I say I'm going somewhere for a couple of days. Because of Milan's tender disposition toward me leaving, I resorted to packing secretly and hiding my suitcase until I was ready to make my getaway. This helped to some extent, but she still knew I was leaving. I also told everyone not to discuss my travel plans in her presence and to spell certain words she knew. I'm not exaggerating. Her ears perk up at the words "leaving," "going away," and "packed." Then she settles into a morose mood, moping around and looking so sad I hate myself for leaving her.

The first time I was able to take Milan with me, you should have seen the celebration. I purchased a travel bag for her and had her teachers at Good Dog train her at school to stay in it. After I packed, I took out her bag and set it next to my suitcase. Milan began cavorting around the bedroom. She dashed over to her toy box. Retrieving her favorite teddy bear, she dragged it over to her travel carrier and pushed it into the mouth of the bag. She was packing too.

At the airport she sat like a little princess in her bag, not moving, a model of perfect behavior. Passersby commented on how good she was, and she gracefully accepted all compliments. During the flight, she slept in her bag underneath the seat in front of me until we landed. When I opened her bag she looked at me as if to ask, "Are we there yet?" Inside the hotel room she sniffed around in excitement and then went straight to the Piddle Pad I spread out for her, assuring me there would be no accidents in the room. The entire trip she was on her best behavior. I think she decided that if she was good she would get to go again. And she did, becoming my constant little escort.

Fast forward to Matisse. When he was finished with school I decided to test him out on a short trip and see how he would do. I handed Milan's travel bag to my assistant and traveling companion, Jennifer, and decided I would commandeer Matisse myself since he was a bit feistier. Sure enough, his instincts against being contained kicked in, and he would have none of me closing his bag. Which was fine until we got on the plane. We got caught in a traffic jam on the way to the airport, which didn't leave enough time for us to buy airline tickets for the dogs. Since I've always rebelled against the concept of paying for what would otherwise be considered hand luggage I have to confess I voted for smuggling them onto the aircraft. Which would have worked if we only had Milan, who never made a peep on the plane or elsewhere.

The moment we got settled in our seats with Milan and Matisse safely tucked beneath the seats in front of us, Matisse yelped his protest at being shut in.

"Arf!"

I tapped on the top of his bag, trying to shush him.

"Arf!" he yelped again.

I cracked the top of the bag and dropped in a treat to silence him. That was my big mistake. The silence lasted as long as the treat did. He yelped again. Now he was on to me and continued blackmailing me for his silence. Needless to say, when I ran out of treats the gig was up. He yelped. I tapped the top of the bag. Fearing the irritation of my neighbors, I opened the top of the bag and allowed him to poke his head out. That spurred him on to wanting to wriggle completely free and sit in my lap, which is not allowed on the plane.

By now Jennifer, sitting across the aisle looking at me, was obviously thinking, *Better you than me!* I was beginning to break out in a sweat. Just about that time we landed. A woman across the aisle said, "Your puppy did so well."

"No, he didn't!" I replied.

To which she answered she had thought so. I said to her, "He didn't do as well as his sister." She was surprised to know I had another dog on the plane. "Exactly my point," I asserted.

And that was just the half of it. I had always been able to take Milan to where I was speaking with no problem. She would wait patiently for me in the room assigned to her, napping and playing with her toys until I was finished speaking. If others were in the room they were quick to comment on how well behaved she was in my absence.

Not Matisse.

The room I left them in while I spoke was in earshot of where I was speaking. Matisse could obviously hear me…and I could hear him barking. My assistant went to play with him. One of the ladies from the church who loved dogs went also. But he would not be comforted. He wanted me…and only me. For a few moments he was distracted with his other passion—food. But then Jennifer ran out of food, and he turned his attention back to my voice.

To be so close and yet so far pushed him over the edge. He whined. Then he scratched at the door. He couldn't bear not being on the other side where I was. He hated not having access to me when I was obviously only steps away. A part of me wanted to go and rescue him, to bring him where I was, but I knew I couldn't. I would just be enabling his bad behavior. He needed to learn to wait.

Paws to Reflect

Ouch! Perhaps waiting is what God is after when I'm busy clawing for what I want. Though it may be close, it is not time yet. And still He waits for me to surrender and depend on Him, trusting His timing for my life.

The stress of fighting to focus on my message and keep the distraction of Matisse's struggle at bay wore me out. I felt sorry for him, yet I was determined to develop his good character. I was there; I was just not within reach. I was within earshot, but I wasn't cooperating with his agenda. He had to get to the place where he could accept that. He needed to learn who was boss. This required tough love on my part, not giving in to his whims no matter how much he whined.

I'm sure God's heart is pulled toward us as He watches us strain in our uncertainty of His plans for us. He reaches out saying, "Don't you know I will never leave you or forsake you? Fear not."

Yet in spite of what we know intellectually of His good intentions, what we don't know—the when, the where, the how—wins out and fear often undermines our trust and faith. I was in agony at the thought of having to get back on the plane with Matisse to go home. I looked at him with a sad heart as he happily greeted me when I was finished. I wanted to be able to take him with me on future trips, but he wasn't ready for the world.

Some of us aren't ready for the world either…or marriage or promotion or fame or anything other than what we presently have. We, like Matisse, are clueless as to what our lack of discipline has caused us to lose. There have been instances where I've envied others who had opportunities I didn't, those who have gotten to go where I wanted to go. Others have been promoted to lofty heights I wanted to achieve. I've complained to God and wondered why He didn't allow me to do the things I felt I was ready to do. "Let me at 'em," I've said. "I could do that without imploding like them." And God has simply said, "That's what you think, but I know better."

I hate it when He does that, but He knows the truth. We don't know the depths of our own capacity to lose it when life gets heady. We think we can handle success, fame, love, and whatever well, but who really knows until in that position?

"The heart is deceitful above all things and beyond cure. Who can understand it?" as the prophet Jeremiah said. It harbors stuff that would shock us if pressed to expose itself. Perhaps that's why we're warned not to think too highly of ourselves lest we fall prey to deception, lose our foothold on good character, and hurt or destroy ourselves and all we hold dear.

I so totally get it now! *God's prevention* is *God's protection*. It's like when I'm walking Milan and Matisse and know I can only allow them to roam free in an enclosed or limited area where they are within my reach. They don't understand…but I do. And I think that's how God see us too. We don't get it…but He does.

This is important to know because sometimes we wonder why we don't go further in life. Perhaps it's because God knows we couldn't handle the places we want to go. Maybe we would embarrass Him or hurt ourselves. Again a spoiled kid in a store comes to mind, raising a ruckus and the ire of every observer while the attending parent tries to look unfazed although dying quietly inside.

Yes, others do behave badly because they haven't developed the character to handle what they've been given access to. We see it all the time. Just watch any of the news or gossip shows on television or read the front cover of the rags at the grocery store. Bad behavior is alive and well. Spoiled rich kids and crazy adults with no excuse for their behaviors. We see these things, shake our heads, and wonder exactly what about that type of behavior is supposed to be cute and attract our respect? Don't they know what they're doing is unacceptable and will be harmful long-term? After the headline has been grabbed and they've savored their 15 minutes of fame, the damage control usually takes much longer and will haunt them for years.

In my own life I look back on situations I found myself in when I wasn't ready to either step up to the plate or appreciate what I had. The opportunities I've blown. The money I wasted. The things I said and wished I could take back. I know I did myself a favor the day I prayed a simple but dangerous prayer: "Lord, please put a halt to anything in my life that would ultimately cause me to be separated from You. If You know that something will make me lose my mind or my soul, please don't allow it to come to fruition."

I said it; I meant it.

But sometimes I wonder if I hadn't prayed that prayer where I would be. What a mess I would have made of my life by now since I certainly don't have amnesia about the messes I made before entering a relationship with God. I know my heart and my tendencies and my weaknesses. Sometimes when I want to do better I actually do worse. Like the apostle Paul, the things I want to do I don't do. And the things I don't want to do, I find myself doing. And that's when I see the wisdom of God. I'm glad He keeps saving me from myself and the stupid moves I'd surely make. And in those times when I chafe against being contained I remind myself that not now doesn't mean never.

18

The Safety of Trust

Training a dog to walk on a leash is fascinating. At Milan's school they told me I should never allow her to walk ahead of me. She is supposed to walk at my heel so she always feels protected by me. To allow her to run ahead of me is to put her in danger. Someone could kick her, she could be attacked by another dog, she could get hit by a car. There are consequences to running ahead of the master.

Milan responded well to this training, walking obediently beside me. Matisse, who is always idling on high, has a hard time, wanting to sprint ahead in spite of my deliberate pace. I'm reminded of the crucifixion every time I walk them. Here I am in the middle, arms outstretched in two different directions, caught between two wayward dogs. Matisse lunging ahead of me in search of a social experience and too distracted to do his business. Milan sauntering willy-nilly behind me, stopping to sniff everything in sight. Every walk is an act of sacrifice. Sometimes I wonder who is walking whom!

And I know I've done the same thing to God. I've dragged Him through my life like that, insisting on going my own way. But even when I'm going in the wrong direction He hangs on for dear life…for *my* life. The resolve that where He leads me I will follow is sometimes a distant memory as I run after my goals and dreams. Again the real issue is not so much my willfulness as it is my ability to trust that He will lead me to the place I really want to be. I should know better by now, but I still find myself playing tug-of-war with God from time to time.

Milan is also very opinionated about where she wants to walk.

When I'm trying to lead her to a place where she can find relief and do her business, she digs in her heels and pulls against my leading. There I stand on the sidewalk trying to pull her without hurting her to a place that I know will better suit her needs. Time and time again we go through this exercise, and I wonder when she will trust me enough to know I'm leading her to the place she really wants to be. She's going one way, and I'm going another. No progress is made, and what she really wants is delayed until she gives in to my direction. Somebody has to lead; someone has to agree to follow, cooperate, whatever you want to call it in order to move forward together. How can two walk together unless they agree? That is the question for every relationship—marriage, friendship, boss to employee.

Trust is crucial to any relationship. Sometimes we have to trust even when we don't have all the information. To trust in the intentions of the one that we love, the one we serve, or the one who serves us. If the person loves you, respects you, or cares for you, his or her plans toward you are for good and not for evil.

I want to lead Milan to green pastures, but she doesn't know it. Matisse doesn't either, so he piddles in mid sprint. One leg up in the air, spraying as he goes because he can't wait until I get him to a good spot. Aren't we like that? Grabbing moments of gratification, such as empty calories and needless appetizers, because we don't know when the real meal is coming? By the time it arrives we don't appreciate the richness of what has been prepared for us because we're too full of junk, including baggage from past relationships and offenses from situations we set ourselves up for and refuse to own.

🐾 Paws to Reflect 🐾

In order for any relationship to work, whether it be human to human, human to pet, or human to God, trust is what makes the union fruitful. Two souls cannot move forward together if there is no trust. If one can't or won't yield to the other's decision functioning as a unit breaks down and can put the entire relationship in jeopardy.

I'm insulted when my attempts to do something for Milan (or anyone for that matter) are met with resistance because my direction or motive isn't trusted. God probably feels the same way. God wants me to trust Him so He can lead me to pleasant streams and places that will restore my soul. He wants me to trust Him to lead me to the places He knows I ultimately want to go so He can bless me with the things I've been longing for. I need to trust Him so that I don't draw back in fear and refuse to follow. I need to trust Him so I don't rob myself of His blessings and then turn around and blame Him for withholding the desires of my heart. When we discover that the safest place we can dwell is in God's shadow, the temptation to stray will cease to be. Only as we choose to surrender to His leading will our desire to wander be changed to contentment to stay.

SoundBite
The Freedom of Limitations

Many times what I assume will be just another walk with my "puppas," as I call them, turns into an adventure. Like the morning I looked death in the face.

It was a crisp day that started off well enough. Milo spent the night and now he and Milan were ready for the world. For variety, I decided to take a different route for our walk. To avoid being yelled at by the yard-Nazi across the street, I struck out for a plot of grass that was kitty-corner to my building. After pressing the pedestrian crossing light and waiting for it to light up, we began making our way across the street. All of a sudden Milo decided he didn't feel like going that way. He dug in his heels in the middle of the street and refused to go further. Meanwhile Milan was sauntering ahead. The light was blinking, signaling a change, so I tugged at Milo's leash and told him firmly, "Come on, Milo. We've got to get out of the street. This is not the place to stop!"

I thought the urgency in my voice would prod him forward, but it heightened his resolve. He began backing up in the middle of the street. As I pulled the other way, Milo wriggled and pulled against me until suddenly he was free of his new collar. He bolted just as the cars began to move impatiently forward, their drivers anxious to get to work on time. I lunged forward, trying to decide which one was easier to face: death by oncoming traffic or death by Milo's mother.

How could I tell her that her beloved child was hit by a car on my watch. No, I would have to move quietly to a foreign country. There was no way I could conceive of delivering this horrendous news. So I did the only thing I could think to do. I *screamed*. I yanked Milan up with one arm and dashed wildly after Milo, managing to grab him in mid-swerve. I scooped him up in my other arm and ran across the street.

I didn't know who was shaking most, me or poor Milan, who had never heard me raise my voice before. Poor thing. She was completely traumatized, and so was I. Milo, however, looked as if it was all in a day's walk. As I slipped on his collar and grabbed his leash in a death grip instead of a casual grasp, Milo looked at me askance and then followed obediently. He got the message. I meant business. No more waywardness would be allowed.

Fast forward to the present day. I've had to apply myself to retraining Milan and Matisse on the leash. My recent leniency caused them to lapse on taking my authority seriously. I said "come," and they looked at me as if trying to decide if they wanted to or not. Walks had become disorderly, with each dog wandering willy-nilly, often pulling me in opposite directions. Sometimes Milan decided she didn't feel like walking at all. So back to school we all went.

Once again I had to submit to a talking-to from John, Marilyn, and Howard about who was the boss and how to make that clear to Milan and Matisse. Back on went the pinch collars. Instantly I had two of the most obedient dogs on the planet, walking serenely and respectfully beside me. Why did it come to this? Because "what is not corrected goes unperfected." I now had to instill the basic rules in them all over again.

We've all heard "Give some people an inch and they'll take a mile." Because I wasn't consistently correcting Milan and Matisse, they assumed their behavior was fine. And this is the case with any relationship. We can't expect people to respect our boundaries if we've never established or enforced them. We can't be offended when they break rules they never knew existed. At the end of the day people (and dogs) feel better when they know the limitations. There is great freedom in understanding which lines we shouldn't cross.

God is very clear on the boundaries He's set for us so we can enjoy a great relationship with Him, as well as other people. Yet often the silence of God, as well as that of people in our lives, gets misinterpreted as approval, which leads us to exercise our misinterpreted liberty, opening the door for the consequences of stepping outside God's plan. When God corrects us, we often strain against the reproof, bolting from the correction or change demanded. And yet it's the voice of God—and God alone—that can lead us to safety. Every time I run from it, I face death. The death of a relationship, of hope, of effort. I've watched my own futile efforts come to naught when I ignore His instructions.

God's words haunt me, "My sheep listen to my voice; I know them, and they follow me" (John 10:27). And yet so often I follow my own voice, the voice of my peers, my desires, my flesh. I find myself staring at the wreckage caused by my foolish actions. And class begins again. My stubbornness must be crucified all over again. I'm miserable until I discover the safety of surrender to my Lord, Jesus.

19

The Price of Prejudice

Shortly after I returned from Ghana, where I spend the Christmas holidays with my dad, I noticed something different about Matisse. My sweet, cuddly, lovable Velcro baby, as I had come to call him, had become aggressive. Not toward everyone…only toward golden retrievers or other golden-haired, large male dogs.

At first I thought he'd developed a Napoleonic complex toward big dogs since he really thinks he is a big dog. But nope, it's only golden retrievers and the like that make him go ballistic. When we encounter one on a walk, I have to hold tight to his leash and pull him away. He starts off sniffing them tentatively, and all of a sudden he goes into attack mode, much to the surprise of the innocent dog. I was mortified, apologizing profusely to the other dog's parent the first time it happened. Matisse was turning into Bailey, Milan's spurned boyfriend.

Remember how he attacked dogs that Milan was near? Bailey had previously attacked Matisse, sending Milan into even deeper retreat and fear of him. I missed that first attack. I was told Bailey came out of nowhere as Matisse was enjoying a moment of interaction with Hudson the Havanese. All of a sudden there was Bailey with a death grip on Matisse's ear while he yelped for his life.

The second encounter was surreal. I had just stepped off the elevator from a walk with Milan and Matisse when I ran into Bailey's mother. I was holding Matisse in my arms and Milan was next to me, edging behind my legs to avoid Bailey. In the middle of our conversation

Bailey leaped up and nabbed a piece of Matisse's beard. Milan scooted around the corner, not wanting any part of the altercation. After air-lifting Bailey from the side of Matisse's face, we tried to psychoanalyze why Bailey was bent on doing Matisse in. We finally figured out that in Bailey's mind Matisse was the new man in Milan's life.

Now in Bailey's defense, he is a very sweet dog. His walker has no problems with him. It's only when he is with his mother that he goes into protect mode and has issues with other males, human or canine. He was a rescue dog, and it's obvious that something happened in his "before" years that shaped his response to males. Someone made it bad for everyone.

This is what so often happens in life. One bad experience with one person can infect the mindset of someone against an entire group of people, causing that person to develop prejudices and end up penal-izing people who don't deserve it.

One day I got a notice under my door announcing new rules con-cerning pets in my building. After all the curbing and leashing rules, they added that there would now be a pet fee. Every year all the pet owners would have to pay $150 for the first pet and an additional $100 for each additional pet. And we were limited to owning three.

I couldn't wait to find the building manager. *Whose brilliant idea is this?* I thought. Obviously not pet owners. I could understand fines for your dog making a mess in the hallway, but a fee for simply owning a pet? House rental for your pets to stay in a place you already own is unacceptable to me. Wasn't that something covered in the already too high assessment we had to pay?

When pressed for an explanation I discovered that the few people in the building who didn't control their dogs were responsible for all of us now having to pay the price for the sins of their dogs. Argh! This was a tough one. Dog owners can understand how there might be some rare mishap in the hall. And responsible owners immediately clean up the mess. I could never understand why some owners don't feel the need to clean up after their pooches. *Who raised those people and what do their houses look like?* I thought.

I can see how this situation could be highly annoying for non-dog owners. I used to be one myself! They aren't invested in or love the dogs. Without a positive connection and interaction with what or who we are observing, it's easy to give a whole group of people a bad rap because of a few. We do it every day with races, religions, genders, those challenged in different areas, and sexual persuasions. We decide that their differences and their behaviors aren't good because they aren't like us. We begin mandating boundaries they should live within, the rights they should or should not have, or some people outright attack them. And sometimes this isn't blatant…it's insidious.

This came to light in my own life recently. I was scheduled to speak at an event hosted by a ministry that spends a lot of time counseling those who voluntarily come to them for help in sorting out their sexual struggles. I received a letter from a gentleman who had some personal prejudices against this particular ministry. His attitude surprised me. I had only heard good things about this ministry, and as far as I know they have a stellar reputation.

I had another friend who had spoken at this ministry's events regularly who had never witnessed anything that would warrant the criticism this other man was so freely giving. So I called the gentleman and asked him to clarify his concerns.

I told him that sexual issues were not my area of expertise and that my message to this audience would be similar to the ones I give to most general audiences. I invited him to attend the conference and perhaps meet with me there. But he went on and on about how the organization was a sham and how they had never helped anyone. They only destroyed lives. He offered a list of witnesses I could listen to for confirming what he had to say.

I responded that I was sure the organization had their list of successes as well, but those didn't interest him. Still, because of his objections, I felt hemmed in. I sympathized with him, but I also was bound to my commitment. The event was already publicized. After what I thought was a calm and fruitful exchange, we hung up on good terms…so I thought.

Imagine my surprise a few days later when I got a call from a producer at a TV station where I regularly appear on the morning news as a relationship expert. This producer informed me that they were terminating my appearances.

The man I'd spoken with on the phone had put one of his friends up to writing the station to ask why they had me on the air when I endorsed a ministry he felt was prejudicial and damaging to people. This letter had been sent to one of the anchors and then passed on to an executive producer.

Needless to say, all the powers that be had their hair on fire. No one wanted any trouble, so they dropped me to avoid stirring up controversy. I scratched my head and wondered what had become of free speech. What happened to the freedom to have an opinion? What happened to being able to agree to disagree? What about "honoring diversity"? This man had written off an entire ministry simply because he disagreed with their mission, their claims of success, and their methods. He was judging them and discriminating unjustly.

Now I was offended. First, I was being accused of something that wasn't true. Of something that went against my personal principles on a deep level. Second, if anyone knew about the pain of dealing with discrimination it was me. I am a black woman for crying out loud. That's two strikes against me in some circles. Third, in this whole process no one at the studio talked to me about the situation. What my opinion was, what the depth of my association with this group was, where I stood…nothing! I had been kicked to the curb, and no one even looked back to see if I was bleeding.

I was hurt, I was angry, and I found myself teetering on the brink of prejudice because of one person's cruel actions. Ironically, it was the thought of all the people I know and love who struggle with the same issues this ministry is helping people with that pulled me back from falling over the edge of bitterness. The men and women I know are kind, loving, and incredible. They bless my life. They are so unlike this man who obviously had issues of his own that spurred him to his divisive actions.

🐾 Paws to Reflect 🐾

In the past when I've done something I know I shouldn't have done I've sought out someone to make me feel better about myself by affirming that what I did was okay. It didn't always work but it didn't stop me from trying either.

I've learned the hard way that the acid test for me in anything I do is to ask if I have peace about it. If I don't I need to get together with God and work it out. Guilt and conviction are functions of the spirit, not the intellect. Anything that we do that goes against what God has said will always leave us feeling unsettled and ill at ease unless we've hardened our hearts. This is the dis-ease of sin. It can make us ugly and insistent when others won't celebrate what we're doing. Agreeing to disagree or polite tolerance becomes not enough because we *need* someone to make us feel all right about ourselves. And that is nobody else's job really. That is totally between God and the individual. He is the only one who can give us a sense of identity. Your fear of not being right can make you lash out at everyone who is not like you… thus the birth of another level of prejudice that becomes like a religion. And religion can kill in spite of good intentions.

Belief isn't something that can be pushed. Sometimes it's hard for a passionate person to bear the thought that not everyone lines up with his or her opinion. I wish they would but it's just not realistic. As the old folks say, "Everybody's got to walk on their own shoes and pay for their journey."

In the midst of disagreement there needs to be room for everyone to find their way to the place of love and understanding. It's always best to believe that no one is unredeemable…though it might take more time than we want to give some people. Attacking them doesn't get them there sooner, that's for sure. If anything they're sure to run the other way or dig in their heels and demand their own rights to protect their ground. This is where we can get stuck and come to no fruitful end. As a matter of fact, we all lose and die by degrees in some ways because there's nothing life-giving about waging war.

Prejudice is ugly. It spawns accusations, incites hatred, stirs up fear. Love can agree to disagree and cover the offense of the other as many times as it needs to in order to leave room for redemption to do its work.

Somehow sexual sin has become magnified in the church, held up as more offensive to God. But really *all* sin is an affront to God. The book of Galatians has a long list of "works of the flesh" that are not sexual in nature. Have you seen the church mount boisterous campaigns against lying, overeating, gossip, jealousy, drunkenness, hatred, lack of integrity? Why not? Why are these sins so easily explained away or ignored? Picking on those who struggle with sexual temptations and habits belies the fact that so many of us struggle with other things that also don't please God.

This is why we need to resist making blanket statements such as "those people...those black people...those white people...those elitist rich...those poor, uneducated...those gays...those straights... those liberals...those conservatives...those...those...those." You get the point. At the end of the day a "those people" attitude exposes our hearts and where we really live. They magnify our own wrongdoing or lack of conviction.

In my final analysis, I felt sorry for the angry man who sought to bring me down. I suspect this man was uncomfortable with himself and chose to make his personal issue everyone's in a negative way by hurting someone else. Some say that the squeaky wheel gets the grease, but I've found that if it makes too much noise the wheel is simply removed and replaced. The backlash of backing people into corners often pushes them to rebel against everything we stand for, including the good parts. People go on the attack, like Matisse does, because of one bad experience. They shun realistic ways to mend their breaches.

God is not prejudiced. To Him there is no Greek or Jew, male or female. He focuses on the state of our souls. Even then He doesn't wrestle us to the ground and insist on our obedience. He gives us a choice. In the book of Deuteronomy God says, "I have set before you life and death, blessings and curses. Now choose life." We get to choose our own outcome.

God *wants* us to choose the path to life and blessing. But if we don't, He won't force us. For Him the lines of demarcation are much simpler: sinner versus *redeemed* sinner made acceptable by the blood of Jesus. Those who willfully choose to go their own way versus those who choose a personal relationship with Him.

God understands that one can ruin it for many. That's why He made a way for One to make it right for everyone. The greatest choice God gives us is made possible through His Son, who rights all the wrongs and blots out all the injustices we commit against God, against ourselves, and against others. This one choice to accept Christ allows us to overcome our prejudices and restrains God's intolerance of the unholy in us.

He waits until the end of time to execute His final conclusions. Until then He reaches out to everyone with love, inviting us to come and settle our differences with Him. The choice is ours, and we don't get attacked if we make a choice He doesn't agree with. He simply waits…and waits…for us to get over ourselves, see the light, and be transformed by it.

20

The Beauty of Being Different

Author John Gray explains the confusion between the sexes by suggesting that men are from Mars and women are from Venus. Maybe so…but I wouldn't limit it just to *human* males and females. By observing the animal kingdom we get some clues about all males and females and the way we're wired. I wouldn't have believed this until I started noting the differences between Milan and Matisse. Milan is all girl. Prissy and particular, she is fastidious and a perfectionist. She is also a nurturer, very sensitive to the moods of others. Polite and mild-mannered but definitely opinionated.

Matisse, in major contrast to Milan, is all boy. Boisterous, daring, athletic, and needing more attention than Milan. Milan is very much all about having her own space, while Matisse is all about crawling into mine. I'm sure to find Milan either at the foot of my bed or on the floor on her favorite teddy bear in the morning. I can also be sure to find Matisse curled up under my left arm. He has the tendency to migrate from the other end of the bed to crowding me by morning. If he isn't curled up next to me, he's sure to be snuggling next to his sister until she pushes him away. He always wants to be touching somebody.

Even when it comes to using the bathroom the differences are obvious. Milan will meander to the piddle station, calmly enter it, find a fresh spot (she would never do it in the same spot twice) and do what she has to. When we go outside Milan is very efficient about finding a spot right away. Though both of them are definitely creatures of habit, Milan has to find a fresh spot in the same vicinity. This mission accomplished, she's ready to go back inside and curl up for a good nap. Matisse has to walk a while, check out the scenery, socialize, and burn off some energy before he focuses on relieving himself. This means we have to walk around two blocks (much to Milan's annoyance) before he focuses on doing his business. If another dog happens by, Matisse is easily distracted, which means we walk around *another* block. If we're in the house he will dash from one room to the other, as if in search of the right spot to piddle. Then he suddenly remembers where he is supposed to go and makes a mad dash to the piddle station to relieve himself. He throws back his head and sighs as if to say, "Thank heavens, I made it."

On a walk, Milan wants to stop and sniff everything in sight and then sit for a while and bask in the breeze. Matisse is focused on charging through life, head held high, unwilling to miss out on any action. It doesn't matter where he's going as long as it's somewhere. He is large and in charge.

The other area that Milan and Matisse differ is how they socialize. Milan is much more reserved than Matisse. In Matisse's mind, if you don't know him you *should...*and he will make sure that happens. On our walks he insists on meeting everyone who wanders by. He accomplishes this by digging his heels into the sidewalk until anyone walking toward us gets close enough for a friendly pat. Milan, on the other hand, is much more discriminating in her choice of who she will interact with, dog or person.

Matisse, although two years younger than Milan, is also her self-appointed protector. This became clear the day Milan and Milo had a little spat. Milo snapped at Milan, and Matisse let him have it. Milo is bigger than Milan and Matisse put together, but Matisse had no fear. He was protecting his big sister.

🐾 Paws to Reflect 🐾

Matisse's desire to protect reminds me of my own brothers and how secure I feel when they are around. They are my protectors, and so are my male friends. I also think of a time when the lines between the sexes were not so blurred, before unisex and androgyny were in fashion. People seemed to have a better grasp on who they were and what their roles were. I long for the days when men were men and women were women.

Don't get me wrong. I'm not referring to the ideology of "me Tarzan, you Jane," but there seems to have been a time when people didn't bump into one another's identities as much and they danced together better. Now many men are confused as to what their roles should be, and women resent the men's lack of confidence. While women are becoming more aggressive to make up the great divide, the chasm widens as men recoil from the reminder of what they're supposed to be. The end result? Countless relationships are in a state of flux. Women wish men would be the strong men they've always longed for because they're weary from pulling the weight they were never created to carry. Men resent being fearful of women, wishing for times when they can really feel masculine and use their natural inclinations to lead, protect, and provide for their families. All of this gets buried as we squabble over our rights and ignore the natural design of who we were created to be and the benefits when we embrace that design by God.

In spite of how the world redefines gender roles, we can't go against the grain of how we were divinely designed without some serious repercussions. The conflict we feel in our souls will keep us in a perpetual state of turmoil until we get back to the basics of who we really are.

What's intriguing about Milan and Matisse's interactions is the undercurrent. Matisse fancies himself the alpha dog and is always trying to assert his dominance. Milan humors him…until he crosses the line, and then she firmly puts him in his place. If you didn't know better you would think she is passive–aggressive. But no, she's simply a female. She picks her battles, putting up with his antics until he finds her last nerve and tweaks it. She responds by pinning him to the floor and letting him know she's had enough, and she could beat him if she wanted to. See? Total female.

It's true. Men and women really are different. And this is a good thing. We need one another. We balance one another. And when we learn to celebrate our differences instead of seeing them as handicaps, that's when the real adventure begins. Much has been written about male and female energy. How polar opposites create a positive force, and how that can't happen when everyone insists we must all be alike. Men and women should be treated with equal respect, but we simply can't all have the same roles. A world in which both genders are alike would be pretty boring. The animal kingdom must instinctively understand this because animals are very clear on who they are…even if we humans are still trying to sort it out.

By instinct animals sense one another's strengths and weaknesses. The big dogs are gentle with the little dogs, being careful not to overpower them. It's beautiful to watch. Standing in the middle of a dog park it becomes clear. We can all get along even though we're different. Here I stand watching pugs, golden retrievers, pomeranians, labs, terriers, and shih tzus all playing together. No one is trying to best the other. They are cavorting and genuinely enjoying their freedom, the sun, the wind, and one another's company. Each of them is distinctly diverse. Yet here they are—hunters, house dogs, guard dogs—all laying aside their differences in pursuit of the enjoyment of the moment.

Perhaps if our goal at the end of the day was to pursue peace and joy instead of forcing others to be just like us, we would all be more comfortable. We would be free to celebrate our differences and discover how they can contribute positively to everyone.

21

The Big Picture

One day when we were at the park a man was throwing a ball for his terrier to retrieve. Milan got really excited and ran the length of the park and back with the terrier. After three laps she figured out that if she only ran halfway he would meet her on the way back, so she parked herself and waited for his return. True to her nature, she is a house dog. When we left the park, the retriever was still busy...well, retrieving. It made sense. His owner was an athletic guy. He needed a more active dog. I did not.

Once when Milan and I traveled to Atlanta one of my friends, Terri, asked if she could take Milan home with her while I was speaking at an event. Her husband, Alan, attempted to take Milan jogging. After half a block he gave up and brought her home, commenting that she didn't run very fast. Between the extreme summer heat and the experience of being pushed beyond her usual capacity for exercise, poor Milan was totally traumatized. By the time she came back to me she was throwing up and suffering from diarrhea. A retriever and runner she was not. And yet she perfectly serves her purpose in my life. She doesn't need to hunt, fetch, or be athletic to please me. Her job is to look cute, be playful, and love me.

Each of us possesses different strengths, is driven by different motives, but collectively we all contribute to the big picture of this thing called life. This is how some of our needs get met—through different sources. In some strange, incomprehensible way we're all connected, and together we make the world go around. Perhaps that's why God compares us (believers and the church as a whole) to a body with all the parts working together. The strong bearing the infirmities of the weak, taking up the slack so we all win together. What a team!

Quite some time ago I was in physical therapy for my knee. After several surgeries I was having trouble getting my knee to bend. Whenever the therapist bent my knee I would grow faint. I asked about this and was told that when a part of the body gets hurt the blood rushes from every other area to assist the wounded part in getting better. Wow! Think what it would be like if people did that. If we all rushed to assist one another when our well being was threatened. Can you imagine what would happen? Sadly, humans instead have the reputation for killing their wounded instead of nurturing them back to health.

The day Milo snapped at Milan and Matisse came to her defense, Milo snapped back at Matisse. Big mistake. Instantly Milan and Matisse became a pack. They were immediately unified. Two little rear ends were poised in the air, tails flailing as they crouched side by side, telling Milo off good and proper. Milo backed off as they doubleteamed him. At the time it was pretty hilarious watching brother and sister unite when they were usually getting on one another's nerves. Their differences dissipated in the face of a common threat. An hour later Milan would be chasing Matisse again in irritation, but for now they had each other's back.

🐾 Paws to Reflect 🐾

The apostle Paul wrote to the church, "The body is a unit, though it is made up of many parts; and though all its parts are many, they form one body…Now the body is not made up of one part but of many…God has arranged the parts in the body, every one of them, just as he wanted them to be" (1 Corinthians 12:12,14). This keeps our significance from getting blown up into self-importance. For no matter how significant we are, it is only because of what we are a part of—God's family.

This is the divine balance God set in the universe. Like all those different dogs at the park, each one suiting the needs and temperaments of his or her master, we too are all needed for different functions to please God and fulfill His purpose in the world according to what He needs from us individually and collectively. If God needs us to complete His plan, how much more do we need one another to have the best possible quality of life?

According to scientific research bees are responsible for one out of every three bites of food we eat because most plants require pollination. Bees ensure the production of seeds in most flowering plants. So we would end up starving if it weren't for tiny little bees! And yet I don't hear them screaming to be recognized. They just do what they do, buzzing along, creating a song in harmony with the universe. This is a powerful principle.

We all play a part in furthering and enhancing life in one another, each with distinct roles that don't always seem important. Nevertheless they are in the overall scheme of things. No one is unimportant in the mix, no matter how weak or strong, because we all bring something to the table of life. We all have something to offer that brings balance to God's creation.

So, though we are all different, there is no excuse for not loving and respecting one another, for not pressing past the things that could divide us. After all, we all want the same things at the end of the day, don't we? To live, love, be loved, and bask in the sun.

How delightful and sad that it takes animals to show us how this should be done. Charge that to God's sense of humor.

22

The Importance of Lingering

Every time I have a gathering at my house I can be sure to witness comic moments between Milan and my guests. If they're visiting for the first time, I clue them in as to what they can expect. For one thing, Milan works the room, checking out each visitor. So I tell them that their approval ratings will rise or fall based on whether or not they give her a tummy rub. Coyly sidling up to them Milan will stop to check them out, sniffing, circling, sniffing. The moment they turn their heads her way, she rolls over on her side and awaits a massage. Several of my guests have been a bit befuddled by this, and I've had to explain again, "She's waiting for you to rub her tummy."

"Oh!" they squeal in delight and enthusiastically bend to appease her. They always pat or stroke her for a moment and then straighten up to continue their conversation, but Milan stays in the same spot, not moving. You see a *pat* is not enough. She wants you to rub her tummy as if you *mean* it. As if it's a priority and serious business.

For her this is not just a "flash in the pan" moment of pleasure; it's how she connects with people. When they take the time to give her a serious tummy rub, bonding happens. Milan makes no bones about it! Quality time begins with touching one another, slowly and deliberately for as long as it takes until a connection is made. If it gets really good for her, she will roll slowly, lifting her leg and indicating to them where she wants to be rubbed next, as if to say, "Over here...yeah, that's it." Oh, you better believe it! She will give you a course in tummy massage.

Systematically she moves around the room from person to person until everyone has had the opportunity to share this experience. My guests all go away the better for it, smiling a little broader than when they first arrived. Milan has woven her magic once again.

Matisse works the room differently. Going from person to person, he stands up on his hind legs and motions to them with one of his front paws, tapping the person playfully until he or she pays attention. He never takes no for an answer and won't move on until my guest has completely tussled his hair and given him the proper attention he seeks. When satisfied, he moves on to the next person.

Milan and Mattise both know what they want and are not ashamed to ask for it. And guess what? *They get what they're looking for.* I think we can all take a lesson from them. The first one is to know what we really want. Sometimes that's the hardest part—being in touch with ourselves.

I was in London recently for a speaking engagement that was both fulfilling and exhausting. As I tried to balance my speaking life with my social life, I think I imploded. I had so many people I wanted to see and far too little time. By the time my trip was ending I felt as if I'd run a marathon, but I'm not exactly sure where I had run to. As I crammed my visits to all my loved ones into my crazy schedule, my heart never settled into a real conversation with anyone. At the end of the trip I had collected the facts on what everyone was up to, but there hadn't been enough time for a true heart-to-heart exchange. I felt as if every visit was unfinished. I felt unresolved.

As I hugged the last people goodbye, they burst into tears, so sad to be parting. I was mortified. I'd missed it. I'd missed taking the time to be silent and just be with my friends. To really *feel,* not just hear, what they were saying. A few of them had been lying on their sides like Milan does, and I didn't have enough time to massage their faith, their pain, their questions. To really get down to the nitty-gritty with them. Transparency and vulnerability got lost under mere surface observances. So much for having an efficient schedule. I had accomplished nothing…nothing that really mattered.

I wished my friends had been more like Milan, who doesn't allow me to get distracted when we're bonding over a tummy rub. She lies content, but the moment I stop she swats my hand as if to say, "Hey, you're not finished 'til I say so!" And I obediently comply until she rolls over and walks away. She doesn't release me until she is released from…well, whatever a good tummy rub releases her from.

Paws to Reflect

When God tells us to laugh with those who laugh, weep with those who weep, and mourn with those who mourn, that sounds well and good. But the problem is that it takes time to sit and feel what people feel, to get into their heads, their hearts, their souls. More time than most of us are willing to give. It can also be a bit scary because it demands that we press into one another and get naked, get vulnerable.

It always amazes me how Milan feels no shame at totally exposing herself for a good tummy rub. But that's the only way she would get what she's seeking. She exposes herself without apology. She's got nothing to prove and everything to gain. Sometimes I wish I could be that open. That relaxed about others seeing my need. Or me seeing theirs. Sometimes the needs of others make me uncomfortable. I become embarrassed by their personal exposure…and yet there's that whole "we are all a part of one body" truth. We all need one another. And God made us that way on purpose. If we could only focus on the beauty versus the shame of being naked we could all be more bold about sharing our need to be touched, of being honest about what hurts and where we need balm applied.

One of my London friends did speak up about my lack of time. He said, "You know, next time you come it would be nice to make the time to have you over for dinner and get you away from all of this so you can relax." I got the hint. He'd felt my attention was divided, and he was right. In the middle of our conversation another friend arrived. I was torn between allowing my friend to finish a personal story and not keeping the other person waiting because she had driven a long way to see me.

That wasn't the only time that happened. I realized that friendship takes time. *All* relationships take time. The kind of time that allows us to communicate with words *and* from the heart through a smile, a touch, a sigh, perhaps in silence until we know the visit has accomplished its purpose. We need to experience one another. Becoming deeply intimate in an organic sort of way through time spent lingering. Lingering until we've both had enough.

I think Jesus was that way. I'm sure others considered Him a bit intense. He was always searching their souls as He looked at them. There was healing power in His touch. In His clothing. In everything about Him. And He always took the time to linger until everything that needed to be accomplished was completed. He was never in a hurry. Going out of His way to visit some that no one else had the time of day for, He took His time with every divinely appointed exchange and left no one the same for the time spent together.

I so want to be like that. Making every moment with everyone I encounter count. I'm a touchy-feely person, but society teaches us to limit this lest our intentions are misread. But I wonder if anyone would really mind if I touched them. Touched them where it counts, in their hearts. I don't think so. And yet I hesitate. Perhaps what I really fear is what they will discover about me. It's not so much about their nakedness, but mine. Because every touch demands an exchange that sometimes I'm not ready for. Sometimes the discovery of what the other person needs from me is overwhelming or calling for more than I have to give. When this happens, I often feel as if I've failed. But I know I haven't…because I know I should always leave room for God to work. Even so, sometimes guilt and sadness overtake me in these instances when I feel I haven't measured up.

When I look at Milan and Matisse throwing themselves with total abandonment into the arms of others, I covet the freedom to celebrate my needs rather than being ashamed of them. Perhaps then they would be met more readily. Perhaps they would be smaller than they seem if I exposed them more often for others to see and touch.

Do you feel this way at times? I think it's all part of learning how to get back to the garden, to the Eden we wandered away from. The garden where man and woman were both naked and unashamed. Where life was perfect because no one had learned how to hide yet.

I'm purposing to make my way back there, touch by touch.

23

The True Meaning of Intimacy

Milan wasn't herself.

That was obvious. She wasn't interested in going out for a walk. No way, no how.

I was away on a trip and had left her in the care of Milo's mom, Annette. She told me that Milan refused to go outside with Milo and Matisse. Instead, she turned around and headed back down the hallway to sit at the door of my apartment.

I arrived home later that night. Just as I was about to head for Annette's, she called saying, "You need to come and get Milan. I think she's sick. She just wet the bed in her sleep. And now she's just lying there." Milan never did that.

Annette thought perhaps she had another seizure.

A month or so earlier Milan had been out walking with Annette. On their way home, when Annette got to the end of the hall, she looked back and didn't see Milan. She went back around the corner and there was Milan, lying on her side, stiff and unseeing. When Annette called her she finally responded and slowly made her way home.

I had taken Milan to the vet, who put her through a battery of tests that revealed absolutely nothing. All I got was a dour admonition to watch her closely for signs of repeat seizures. If they began to occur regularly, she would have to be on medication for the rest of her life. I was dumbfounded and upset. I couldn't bear the thought of her suffering and being in pain, but neither could I fathom her having to take medication all the time. She was only three years old, with hopefully at least 13 more years to go. The rest I didn't even want to think about. And now this.

Rushing to Annette's, I scooped Milan up from the bed, cuddling her and holding her close. Off we went to the emergency dog clinic for another round of tests. But there was nothing that indicated she had another seizure. Again I was told to just watch her.

The next day she moved slowly outside to do her business, and after that she laid down on the sidewalk refusing to go any further. I had to carry her home.

I made an appointment with her regular vet, Dr. Schule. After listening to what I had to say, he nodded knowingly. "I think I know what it is." With that he pressed the middle of Milan's back, and she gave a little cry. He scooped her off the table and said, "I'd like to take some X-rays to confirm it, but I think she has a herniated disk."

Once he was sure of the diagnosis, he wrote a prescription and told me she was not to have any heavy exertion or exercise for seven days. I knew she'd love that part. Poor thing. Her back had been hurting, and she had no way of letting us know. She fought the good fight, trying to keep up with the others until the pain became too great and she couldn't bear it anymore.

On another occasion Milan kept having problems with her right eye. The doctor said she had incurred a scratch on her cornea. I was given drops to give her, and they seemed to do the trick. I say *seemed* because later, after a third recurrence (which was so frightening I had to take her to emergency), it was suggested I take her to an ophthalmologist.

Okay, I didn't know dogs had their own eye doctors until then either. Sure enough, the problem was more serious. Her cornea had been punctured. The drops I'd been giving her had been aggravating the problem because it was healing the surface, but the tear under the surface wasn't being addressed. The doctor changed her prescription, and soon she was as good as new. The doctor commented on how good she was. She never flinched or moved, allowing her to look in her eye like an old pro. I think Milan was in so much pain she was relieved to finally have someone address it. But some of us have the opposite reaction, fearing the touch of the one who can heal us.

One day while I was playing with Matisse, rubbing his tummy and trying to tame his mane, he rolled over and his ears flopped back to reveal blood inside. I was mortified. I dove in for a deeper look, but he kept pushing my hands away. Finally I pinned him on the bed to conduct a thorough investigation. He had been scratching so much that the skin was raw in both ears. Grabbing some cotton I again pushed his paws away to wipe the area clean and apply some ointment to stop the itching. This went on for several days until he seemed to finally understand I wasn't out to hurt him and was helping him get better. Sometimes we have to be willing to press past seeming rejection to see what hurts when it comes to those we love.

🐾 Paws to Reflect 🐾

I felt guilty because I hadn't noticed Milan and Matisse's distress right away. I'd been so busy rushing to and fro I hadn't noticed anything wrong. I purposed to watch more closely and take nothing for granted. Call me an obsessively vigilant mother if you will, but I never want to be insensitive to the pain of Milan, Matisse, or anyone else I love. But sometimes it's not so simple. Sometimes we have to be willing to look deeper when others are trapped in their pain, unable to communicate what and why it hurts.

One day I got in a very heated argument with a friend. I said something very simple that made him go ballistic. He erupted and started shouting at me like a crazy person. My first reaction was to run for cover. I felt his response was over the top and totally unwarranted. I decided I was never going to speak to him again. But later the entire exchange weighed on me so heavily I decided to pray about it.

As I began to pray I got this picture in my mind of a wounded horse. Every time I tried to get close to try to help, it kicked me—but not out of anger…out of fear. Fear of the pain growing greater. I got the message. I called my friend and apologized. I asked him to forgive me for being insensitive to his pain, for missing the cues of how hurt he really was. I told him I would never hurt him deliberately and didn't realize how misunderstood he felt.

His anger was totally diffused. He was able to explain why he'd responded in such a volatile fashion, and we calmly talked about how he felt and got to the root of the problem. Some of his own responses surprised him, and by the time we exhausted the subject he felt moved to reach out to the person the whole argument was centered around in the first place. He'd felt deeply rejected by this person and hadn't taken the time to deal with it. Instead he'd gone into defense mode to subdue his pain. Unknowingly, I had pushed all the wrong buttons and torn the scabs off of his wounds.

Sometimes I imagine God holding me close, checking me for fleas or simply reaching out to touch my wounds and convey His love for me. But I push His hand away because I'm too ashamed of what He might discover. I fear the exposure because I don't know what I'll do with the information. What if it's too overwhelming for me to handle? Or worse yet, a totally unsolvable truth that will deepen my pain? Sometimes I fall prey to the denial that fools us into thinking everything is just fine. And yet what we don't know can do more damage than what we do know. Sometimes the painful truth is the only light that will illuminate the dark corner we're avoiding and eventually light our path to freedom and healing.

Sometimes I'm like Milan, so bound in my pain I simply lie in the middle of it, making a mess with my lack of movement or refusal to share my suffering in a way that would gain me assistance or give me the tools I need to heal. This is not so much out of pride as simply because I can't express my agony or perhaps I think that not even God can really interpret the way I feel. I am rendered speechless. It has always been easier for me to interpret other people's pain than my own. Isn't that how it usually is?

There are times I wish I could step outside of myself and analyze my angst, my fears, my pain from an objective point of view instead of shutting down and wandering through the labyrinth of denial, hoping the torture will stop if I refuse to acknowledge it. But it just grows, digging deeper into the core of my being, where it becomes even harder to uproot.

With prayer, much soul searching, and trusting God more, I'm getting better at keeping shorter accounts of my pain. I've gotten braver over the years at poking my pain. Turning it over. Squeezing it and making it talk to me. I've learned it's better to make friends with my pain and let it whisper the secrets I don't want to hear. Often they hold more truth than I think I can handle. At some point I'm finally ready to listen and acknowledge what God and my body or mind has been trying to tell me. To own my mistakes, misconceptions, bad choices, and the things I need to surrender. And it feels so good to get to that place where my heart finally opens to the healing God is waiting to administer!

I've learned the secret of how to get Milan and Matisse to let me touch their wounds. I get down to their level and then they run to me. As long as I'm standing, towering over them, they back away, rebelling against my perceived dominance. I am fearsome to them in those moments. Too powerful. But when I sit on the floor, they come running, scampering into my arms, reveling in my lap, resting in my arms. And then I can carefully pull and pry as much as I want.

I am loved and trusted because they can hear the beat of my heart.

I believe the same is true of people. People don't want someone talking down to them when they're hurting. They want someone to join them in their pain. To weep with them. To hurt with them. To sometimes say nothing but commune with them. God understands us. Instead of towering over us in heaven, He came down to us. Yes, Jesus came down to our level. He walked where we walk. Suffered what we suffer. Was tempted like we are tempted. Was misunderstood, unappreciated, lonely, betrayed, hungry, cold, and broken just like us. He says, "I understand because I've been there. I love you. I'll help you."

I've heard Him say those words to me. Years ago I was hit by a car and hurt badly. I was incapacitated for over a year, required three operations, and had to learn to walk normally again. When my case finally made it to court, the jury was totally unsympathetic because the defense made the case that after I was hit I wrote a book and created a whole new life for myself, so I didn't need any money for suffering or time missed from work and life.

In the minds of the jury members my life looked too fabulous to substantiate my need to be compensated for the year I'd spent suffering. The hours of testimony by my doctor and my therapist chronicling my long, arduous comeback trail fell on deaf ears. The testimonies of those I regularly worked for citing my inability to work was ignored. Even the fact that I might require surgery in later years and my persisting pain meant nothing to them. They were witnessing my ordeal from a distance and couldn't get past the fact that I was now a successful author and speaker who seemed to be living *la vida loca*. In the end I was awarded what barely paid what I had to hand over to the insurance company.

I was devastated. It wasn't the money that upset me, but what it represented. In my mind the signal they sent was that my life meant nothing and the suffering I experienced warranted no recompense. I tearfully shared how I felt with the Lord as I lay in bed weeping. I'm sure I heard Him say, "I know exactly how you feel." And in that moment I knew He *did* understand, and it comforted me. Nothing had changed except that someone was sharing my pain with me. Like the time one of my best friends, Brenda, held me and wept for me after my heart was broken, so broken that I couldn't weep over the pieces. As I sat frozen to the spot, my eyes told her everything I couldn't say. As her sobs echoed around the room I felt fed by her compassion, and her empathy stopped me from being swept out to sea on a tide of bitterness. Somebody cared. The one who broke my heart didn't care, but Brenda did. And in that moment that was enough to save me.

Intimacy...all this touchy feely stuff can be really scary sometimes because the very nature of it insists we all get naked. And a lot of us aren't comfortable with that level of vulnerability. But that's all right. Keep working at being open. And remember: At the end of the day we're all a lumpy mess, and we're in this together.

And perhaps if we expose the many things we've been harboring we'll find out we're not in such bad shape after all. Or so what if we are? We can't fix what we don't own. We can't heal what we refuse to uncover. God won't take action until we invite Him to. In the midst of pushing Him away, like Matisse did to me, we're really screaming inside for God to press in. Press into our pain and set us free. God knows that, and so He keeps coming. Even when we walk away enraged by His Word, convicted by His Spirit, or wounded by church folks and other imperfect representations of Him. He just keeps coming. Bending down ever so gently to let us know we can trust Him with our pain. Trust Him not to laugh at our stupid mistakes, minimize our wounds, or reject our nakedness.

When we crawl into His lap, drawing so close we can hear His heartbeat, we let Him touch us where it hurts until we are free enough to fully give Him our pain. He then replaces it with His love, His peace, His wholeness, His understanding. He saves us from ourselves, which is what we really need in the first place.

SoundBite
The Deception of Appearances

It was a beautiful, balmy New York afternoon. I had been two weeks on the road without Milan and Matisse and feeling a bit guilty about having left them for so long. So I headed off with Annette and Milo for a day of window shopping, determined to pick up some treats for my babies.

After traveling around the world and speaking of the complicated problems humans can have, my heart was melted when Milo showed how happy he was to see me after a whole year of separation. But cuddling with Milo made me miss Milan and Matisse even more, and I couldn't wait to get back home.

As Annette, Milo, and I walked along the streets on the Upper West Side, every little dog caught my eye and reminded me of what was waiting for me back in Chicago. Just as we were winding down our expedition we decided to stop in one last shop. Off-Broadway Boutique beckoned us with an intriguing window display. We couldn't resist, so in we went. After much ooing and aahing, our browse fest came to an end. Just as we were leaving the store an elderly lady was entering with the cutest little shih tzu in her arms. I gave a coo of delight and dove in for a closer look at her baby. "Oh, you remind me of my babies at home," I murmured as I leaned in for a closer look.

At that moment the dog lunged forward. From somewhere I heard a sharp scream. Annette later said it was me. I recall hearing the dog bark and then chaos followed. Suddenly I realized my nose was stinging. Annette, who was already outside the store, looked back at me and gasped, "What happened?"

I stood holding my nose. "I think that dog just bit me!" I took my hand away from my face. It was bloody. I dashed to the mirror. Down the center of my nose was a long, angry gash with blood pouring out of it. "Oh, no! It's really bad! I'm bleeding!" The employees in the store started scrambling. Snippets of conversation swirled in my still-shocked mind. "I'll get some Kleenex." "I'll get some ice." "Hold your head back, dear." By the time the smoke cleared and I was seated, head back, ice against the bridge of my nose, the woman and her dog had vanished.

The ladies in the store went out on the street, looking up and down, but there was no sign of her. I suspect her dog had done this before, and she feared being sued or being deluged with doctor bills. I recall hearing her mumble at some point, "You should ask before you approach a dog." I admit that's true. Because the dog was a shih tzu, and the breed is known for being laid back and friendly, the thought never occurred to me that her dog would be troubled or vicious.

As I sat in the emergency room waiting to be released after getting shots and being issued a prescription for antibiotics, I texted a friend of mine: "Well, here I sit in ER with a scar down the middle of my nose, stinging from shots, slightly in shock. R U sorry 4 me yet?" He shot back, "Nope, not at all. I'm still trying to find the lesson in this." "Hmm," I wrote back, "perhaps the lesson is that just because something is cute doesn't necessarily guarantee it's harmless." He wrote back agreeing with my conclusion and suggested it confirmed his opinion that I should get rid of the new guy I was seeing.

Well, the jury is still out on *that* particular theory. As I reflected on the dog bite incident, I did draw some conclusions. First, the reason I didn't have any inhibitions about approaching the dog was its familiarity to me. I had two shih tzus of my own. I never considered that all dogs in a species are not created or trained alike. No two people or animals respond to the same things alike. The same situation can make one and break the other. I didn't know the history of that dog. And I don't know the history of everyone I meet. Perhaps that's why the King James Bible says, "Lay hands suddenly on no man." Exercise discernment before you embrace or align yourself with anyone. Man or woman, friend or foe, business associate or casual friend. Know who and what you're dealing with before you expose yourself to possibly being taken advantage of or wounded. Due diligence can certainly lower the number of bad experiences, harmful fallout, and wounded noses.

The other lesson that couldn't be ignored was even more important. Don't assume you know what you're dealing with from surface appearances. One of Milan's caregivers kept her at his house while I traveled several times. It seemed like a good thing because Milan wasn't in a kennel. However, I began feeling uneasy about leaving her at his house, though I couldn't really say why so I stopped utilizing his services. To my horror someone recently told me the dog sitter had been arrested. His home was filled with pens of badly mangled pit bulls. After his home was raided it was revealed that he was involved in dog fighting. To make matters worse, the news also reported that he was a registered sex offender. Unbelievable! Appearances can fool us.

I can't tell you which story amused my friends more. My dog sitter was a closet psycho or my nose being mistaken for a treat. One of my friends said, "That'll teach you to keep your nose out of other folks'…or should I say dogs'…business!" I can't say I'm amused at furnishing so many laughs at my expense.

I'm not sure if my nose smarted more than my pride, but I can tell you I've learned my lesson. Dogs who are unknown to me are to be admired from a safe distance unless I'm invited in for a closer exchange or they've proven they are trustworthy. Hmm…I'll leave it to you to decide who I'm talking about here: men or animals.

24

The Path to Perfect Rest

If you ever want to be inspired to sleep, come to my house! Milan and Matisse make sleep look so good you'll want to join them. I've never seen anyone or any animal enjoy sleeping the way they do.

Picture Milan sitting somewhere in my vicinity watching my every move. Her eyelids start dropping…slowly. At first she fights the current of her fatigue, but eventually her head begins to slump, and the rest of her body follows in a slow slide to the floor. Legs tucked beneath her and front paws supporting her head like a pillow, she settles in. After a while she will rouse just enough to slowly crawl to her teddy bear, cuddling against it for support as she settles in for REM sleep. The progression almost looks like a stop motion film in overcrank: the slow deliberate roll onto her side followed by a complete rotation until she's on her back, legs stretched out, front paws raised, vulnerable to the elements, naked and unashamed. I giggle.

And then the snoring begins. Deep and loud. Like an old man. So unlike the rest of her personality. I wonder how she can so totally give herself to releasing everything and completely revel in doing absolutely nothing.

Once Milan and I traveled to Oregon to my publishers for a meeting. After Milan made the rounds sniffing all the executives at the conference table, she indicated she wanted to sit on my lap. I scooped her up and two minutes later, in the middle of my deep conversation with the committee, a pregnant pause was broken by the sound of deep snores that seemed bigger than the little body that released them. Amazing! That is complete relaxation. That is rest devoid of worry, fear, or concern about the future. Freedom from all the things that keep you and me tossing and turning at night. All the issues of life, all the struggles, and unresolved situations that follow us to bed each night. On those occasions we often awake the next morning more tired than when we went to bed.

And here was Milan, oblivious to any trouble or struggle. She knew she was loved. She knew she would be fed and cared for. She was secure. She was experiencing rest the way God designed it.

When Matisse first arrived, I noticed he was usually restless for quite some time before he settled in to sleep the way Milan did. He would fall asleep but be back up in a matter of minutes, pace to another spot, flop down, curl up in a ball, and go back to sleep. This pattern of behavior continued until he was completely worn out. Sometimes he would wake up with a start, looking for me as if he feared I would steal away while he was sleeping.

I recall as a child waking up one night to find my parents gone. It was scary. They hadn't gone far, just to the corner to pick something up, but it took me a while to recover and sleep soundly again. I was afraid they would go away without my knowledge and never come back. For a long time I would wake up time and time again, listening in the night silence for hints of their breathing...just checking.

Perhaps that was Matisse's problem. He didn't know me enough yet to trust me. He didn't have enough history to know I would always come back. That I would never leave him or forsake him. This was old hat to Milan, who sits the moment I tell her I will be back, as if to let me know she will be waiting.

Once when I traveled I made the mistake of picking Matisse up from his boarding school late in the evening and taking him to the groomers early the next morning. He was beside himself. He refused to submit to a bath or anything John tried to do. Matisse was upset. I'd left him again, and he was not a happy camper. Therefore everyone was going to suffer. John called, frustration punctuating his speech, as he gave his apologies but very firmly suggested I come and get Matisse and not bring him back until he learned some table manners.

Poor Matisse couldn't stop shaking when I picked him up. It was almost as if he was saying, "Oh Mommy, Mommy! I thought you left me again and weren't coming back!" A week later John relented and called to see how Matisse was and offered to give him a free bath. They've since kissed and made up, but I learned never to take Matisse to the groomers the day after I arrive home from a lengthy trip.

Matisse clearly has abandonment issues. Those who stay behind to watch Matisse when I leave tell me he acts out. I've been told that the minute I leave he chews on things. Also he resists the dog walker and refuses to go outside. He wants to be home when I come back… if I'm coming back.

On my return he's the perfect little angel. Annette called him a little demon, which made me laugh. But I suppose it really isn't funny. I very much want him to behave so that people will be willing to take care of him should the need arise. As time is going by, Matisse is beginning to mellow. He's starting to get the idea that even when I go away, I always came back. He's growing more secure and trusting me. To ensure a good night's sleep, he's taken to lying at the foot of my bed curled up in one spot all night, until the morning when he migrates to my side for his habitual bonding and hugging session.

I also noticed that the more of a routine I follow, the more he calms down. It's important for him to know what to expect. He and Milan are truly creatures of habit who don't like their schedules disrupted. The moment they sense any major shift coming, their stomachs get upset and they get the runs. Milan especially has a body clock I have to admire. Wherever she is, at exactly eight thirty at night she drops on the spot and is out cold. Whether she's in the middle of the kitchen floor, the living room, someone else's house…it doesn't matter. A little timer inside her says, "Okay, honey, drop it like it's hot." That's her bedtime, and she doesn't care what's going on around her.

At exactly seven thirty every evening she and Matisse chase one another back and forth, wrestling until they've both worn themselves out, and then they retreat to their separate corners.

Mealtime must also be on schedule. At exactly five thirty Milan sits by her food bowl and refuses to move until I get the message that it's dinner time. Same thing in the morning. Both dogs are happiest when things work like clockwork. They are most peaceful when order and consistency are in their world. The power of repetition establishes security and allows them to rest. The greater their security, the deeper their rest.

It cracks me up that at home they both go to "their" spots to use the bathroom every day. When we travel I've had to wait until they are at the point of bursting before they will do their business because they are totally confused by the new environment. It's like they're not quite sure they really have permission to cut loose. They look so relieved when they finally go that I laugh out loud.

The first time I left Matisse in my hotel room I think he barked until I got back. But after a few trips he settled in, finally understanding that I was coming back. Now he's a travel weary dog who knows the drill. As I shut the door behind me I say, "I'll be back." He acquiesces and releases me to go forth and conquer.

🐾 Paws to Reflect 🐾

Dogs are known for their faithfulness, but they need us to be faithful too. As they long for our return, our appearance settles their hearts and lets them know all is well.

Whether you suffer from sleep deprivation or insecurity in a relationship or marriage, the upset can always be traced back to the need for trust and security. I can't rest if I'm afraid. I can't rest if I love you and I'm agonizing over whether you love me too. I can't rest if I'm worried about you being with someone else or telling my secrets. I can't rest in a relationship when I'm not sure of the commitment.

A man asked me one day why all the women in his life were so jealous. Not only were they insecure, they were passionate about accusing him of playing around. I asked him what he did to stir up these feelings. He was the common denominator in all of these relationships, so he had to look at himself. Then he admitted he was a flirt. Ah ha! He went on to say how he struggled with jealousy himself. I shared with him how wounded people can hurt other people, and that unfaithful people live in fear of being victims of the very behavior they perpetrate. Cheaters almost always think someone is cheating on them because they are guilty themselves. As the Bible puts it, "To the pure, all things are pure, but to those who are corrupted and do not believe, nothing is pure. In fact, both their minds and consciences are corrupted" (Titus 1:15). I'm talking about *people* here, and for the most part we're all pretty jaded. We have a tendency to superimpose our own character, fears, and past experiences on others and even onto God.

Perhaps my own fears that God will renege on His promise to never leave me or forsake me, to provide all my needs, to be a present help in times of trouble have nothing to do with Him at all and everything to do with me. *I'm* the one who is unfaithful. And because of my own waywardness, I struggle with bouts of faithlessness. My unbelief causes me to toss and turn. It robs me of the rest I long for. I find myself, like Matisse, pacing until I arrive at the end of myself and have no choice but to wait—wait for His Word, wait for Him to prove to me again that He is faithful.

One day I too will know the drill and believe Him because He's always consistent. No matter how dramatic or unsolvable my predicament is, nothing with Him has changed. He is still faithful and never out of my reach. I am never alone, never ignored or forsaken no matter how much I shiver in the cold of my circumstances, no matter how isolated my pain makes me feel. He will be here as He has always been.

In that knowledge I rest.

25

What's Truly Important

Once upon a time I *loved* to travel. Perhaps because I was single, I loved being on the road, loved being gone. When I got back home it was a jolt to go from the excitement of a speaking engagement where people were clearly moved to an empty house that was profoundly silent. It was such a stark contrast and a bit disconcerting. But that changed once Milan and Matisse entered my life. Now when I arrive home...love awaits.

Before Milan and Matisse, I would sometimes extend my stay an extra day just to hang out or meander my way back home. But now when they don't travel with me, I know my little babies are waiting, so I leave for home as soon as my commitment is finished.

I miss them when they aren't around. I can't wait to see them come bounding around the corner of the door at their school. I watch them literally leap over one another to get to me. It's always so hilarious and heartwarming to watch. They literally push one another away in order to get to me first. Talk about feeling the love!

This love fest redeems them in my mind from their attitude when I drop them off at the school. The minute the car comes to a stop, they stand up in the backseat and start clawing the window. They can't wait to see their friends. The moment I open the door Matisse bounds from the backseat to the sidewalk with Milan trying to follow suit, though she is never brave enough to take that leap of faith. But the moment I set her on the ground they both take off, running to the door, sitting but twitching impatiently until someone opens it. The instant the door cracks open they shoot inside without a backward glance. I'm happy they have such exciting social lives when I'm gone, but I'm also a little miffed at the thought that my departure is no longer mourned as it once was.

Ah, but by the time I return it's an entirely different story. Truly love is fickle. Perhaps that's why absence makes the heart grow fonder. Or as my mother said, "You never miss the water 'til the well runs dry." By the time I get home they've had time to reflect on who loves them most, who takes the time to play with them, give them massages that make them sigh with delight, and spoil them rotten. That's right. Me…and *only* me. Although they're fed at the school, I know my love is the gravy. I'm convinced that even their food tastes different when I don't serve it to them. I want to believe they miss me as much as I miss them.

I'm perfectly willing to put my sacrifice where my love is. In order for Milan and Matisse to travel with me, sometimes I have to stay in a different standard of accommodation than I prefer. It's fascinating how the lines of demarcation are drawn when it comes to who accepts pets and who doesn't. With hotels, as well as stores, there are two extremes. All the high-end hotels, ala The Ritz, Four Seasons, Embassy Suites, Omni, Starwood, and Hiltons, for the most part allow dogs. Then there is the middle tier of hotels that absolutely will not accommodate pets. I've often thought since smoking seems to be more damaging to a room than having a pet, and they designate rooms for that, why not for pets? Then there are the hotels, motels, and Holiday Inns that are totally fine with bringing furry members of the family along.

And the stores? Saks, Bloomies, Nordstrom, Macys, Neimans, again all the high-end stores, are fine with pets inside. The little chic, unique boutiques second the notion. But the stores in-between won't even allow a pet in a carrier.

I'm waiting for the day when we will be like France where dogs are free to roam everywhere but the grocery store. You can go to any French restaurant and see a dog sitting politely by his owners while they enjoy their meal. Perfectly normal. I'm glad Chicago has several restaurants that allow dogs on the patio during the summer months. One of Milan's favorite pastimes is going to Hugo's and car watching while I eat. The waiter brings her water, and she is totally happy to check out the scenery and bask in the evening breeze. And wherever there are people to admire him, Matisse is *always* happy to go.

One hotel in particular brought it home for me the sacrifice that love is willing to make. My assistant, Jennifer, and I were going somewhere down south, I don't quite recall where now (perhaps I want to blot it out of my mind). We'd been informed that there was only one little hotel that would accept dogs. I thought, *How bad could it be?* Well, it was pretty bad. It was dank and smelly with no room service. We had to cross over railroad tracks to get food. I spent the whole weekend apologizing to Jennifer. The only thing that made up for it was the food across the tracks was fabulous.

The dogs were happy, I was happy, but I can't say the same for Jennifer, though she weathered the storm well.

Paws to Reflect

I can finally relate to the length people go to in order to be with the ones they love. People have moved across the world, given up their crowns, started wars, all in the name of love. For the longing of wanting to be with loved ones, the most atrocious conditions have been endured.

This kind of love, as strong as it is, pales in comparison to the love that compelled Jesus to leave heaven to redeem His bride—His church, all those who believe in Him and accept Him as Lord—because He wants us to be where He is. As He prayed in the Garden of Gethsemane right before His betrayal, the cry of His heart to the Father was that He wanted to bring us all home. And so He was willing to abide in extremely substandard conditions for the sake of us, His beloved, leaving the splendor of heaven to come to earth, face a horrible death on the cross, and rise again.

This type of sacrificial love transforms us.

And now that Jesus has returned to His home in heaven, He waits for us to join Him, looking forward to that day with great expectation. And then finally He will be satisfied and joyful, no longer separated from the ones He loves because we will be one with Him. I so totally understand that longing.

At the end of the day it's no longer where I have to go and all the things I'll see. I've seen them before, and they are all momentary pleasures. My sights are set toward the constants in my life where my heart is anchored and my soul finds solace. Where I'm surrounded by love and peace.

I finally understand that life doesn't consist of the success I achieve or the things I acquire but rather who others become because of my presence in their lives. It's not about the bones I throw to others, it's about how much of myself I give to them, how much they give to me, and how much we are transformed and uplifted from the exchange.

Now I constantly find myself planning my schedule around getting back to my little munchkins because I know they're waiting for me. When I call the school to check on them their teacher always says, "They know you're on the phone and now they're barking." They anticipate my love, and I anticipate theirs. And when I see their shadows pacing back and forth behind the door to my home, waiting for me to enter, I know I am deeply loved. I know I am truly home.

About Michelle...

Michelle McKinney Hammond, a writer, singer, and speaker who focuses on improving love-driven relationships, is the founder and president of HeartWing Ministries, as well as the cohost of the Emmy-winning show *Aspiring Women.* Michelle is the bestselling author of *The DIVA Principle*®, *101 Ways to Get and Keep His Attention,* and *Sassy, Single, & Satisfied.*

To correspond with Michelle McKinney Hammond, write to:

HeartWing Ministries
P.O. Box 11052
Chicago, IL 60611

email her at heartwingmin@yahoo.com

or log on to her websites

www.michellehammond.com
or www.thedivaprinciple.com

For information on booking her for a speaking engagement, call

1-866-391-0955
or log on to www.michellehammond.com

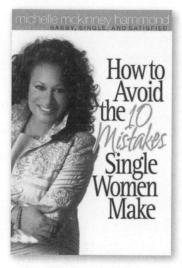

While single women might think their biggest errors have to do with bad first dates, Michelle McKinney Hammond, bestselling author of *Sassy, Single, & Satisfied* (over 200,000 copies sold), addresses the real top-10 mistakes single women make that impact their faith, security, happiness, and, yes, love lives.

With her down-to-earth style, Michelle takes a look at how women unknowingly:

- put life on hold until a man completes the picture
- allow peer pressure to dictate choices and desires
- miss the blessing of each immediate season of life

Through scriptural principles and insightful questions, Michelle helps you examine your outlook and ultimately move toward healthier attitudes and behaviors about men, romance, finances, God, biological clock, and much more.

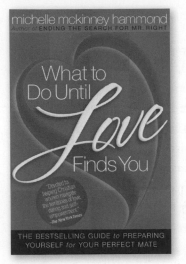

In *What to Do Until Love Finds You,* Michelle offers practical, godly advice on how to

- handle sexual temptations regardless of past experience
- release expectations and embrace life
- get to know God's purpose

The biblical truths, honest personal insights, and refreshing take on love and the single lifestyle will encourage you and help you prepare for true love.

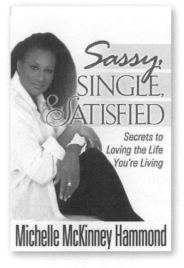

Sassy, SINGLE, & SATISFIED

Secrets to Loving the Life You're Living

Michelle McKinney Hammond

Written especially for you, this user-friendly devotional helps you discover your place in the world and draw closer to the true Lover of your soul. Michelle combines practical scriptural principles for daily living with inspirational stories, quotes, and personal experiences on life, love, and men. Embrace your singleness and celebrate it as you use this life season to grow closer to the Lord. Explore ...

- the best, most fruitful priorities
- how to get the most from being single
- finding joyful and meaningful existence while waiting for a mate

With her humorous, tell-it-like-it-is style, Michelle connects and shares the fulfillment she's found in Christ.

This captivating novel is filled with Michelle's hallmark wit and insight!

Tracy awakens one morning to a radio report—the ratio of eligible men to available women is slim to none. Now armed with actual statistics and a past of heartbreak, Tracey explores with her four good friends how intelligent women with impressive careers, coveted urban dwellings, and closets full of fashions still worry so much about the shortage of men and singleness. As life unfolds they discover surprising truths about love.

Playing God explores the heartache that can come when we try to play God in our lives.

After seven years as a counselor, the once idealistic Tamara Roberts has absorbed so much of the loss, doubts, and trials of her clients that she questions how God can let so much hurt happen in the lives of good people: Corinne Collins' husband, a respected religious leader, has a devastating secret; Lela Deveraux wants to settle a score with her famous husband; Jamilah, Tamara's best friend, goes out on a limb for a young girl. In contrast, Felicia Sample is married, saved, and feeling blessed after a past of indecision and mistakes.

Why are some people blessed? Why is life so hard? And what really remains at the end of the day?

To learn more about Michelle's books
by Harvest House Publishers or to read sample chapters,
log on to our website:

www.harvesthousepublishers.com

HARVEST HOUSE PUBLISHERS

EUGENE, OREGON